The
Fifty Shades of Grey
Phenomena

Chloë Thurlow

YELLOWBAY BOOKS

Published by YellowBay Books Ltd 2012
www.yellowbay.co.uk

YellowBay Books Ltd
9 7 8 1 9 0 8 5 3 0 5 3 0

YellowBay Books is dedicated to edgy,
daring and radical new writing.

Let us know what you think at info@yellowbay.co.uk,
Or visit Amazon and give the book a review

Other books by Chloë Thurlow

A Girl's Adventure

Being A Girl

The Gift of Girls

The Secret Life of Girls

Girl Trade

Flight 69 – The Mile High Club

Sophie's Secret

Laid & Betrayed

www.chloethurlow.com

Contents

Introduction

The EL James trilogy *Fifty Shades of Grey*, *Fifty Shades Darker* and *Fifty Shades Freed* has shown there is a hunger for good erotic fiction, especially among women. What may come as a surprise is that the hunger has *always* been there.

More surprising still, the forms of domination, submission and chastisement EL James depicts in her books are fundamentally the same as those detailed by the Marquis de Sade 200 years ago, and, with variations on the theme, explored through the 20th century by Anaïs Nin, Catherine Millet, Pauline Réage, Anne Rice and many other fine writers.

The original step taken by EL James, the secret of her immense and merited success, is that she has taken romance and made it erotic. She did not take the erotic and add romance. This quintessential difference creates a powerful dynamic tension and a new literature for a new generation.

- ➢ Part 1 of this book is an analysis of the journey made by EL James and a guide to how new writers may follow in her footsteps.

- ➢ Part 2, *The Life of the Marquis de Sade*, provides a biography of de Sade and shows how his work sowed the seeds of the erotic genre as we know it today.

- ➢ Part 3, *The Work of the Marquis de Sade,* includes extracts from his novels *Justine* and *120 Days of Sodom*.

- ➢ Part 4, *Contemporary Erotica,* contains extracts from my own work and tips on writing erotica for a modern audience. It would be useful to include excerpts from EL James's novels, but copyright laws do not permit this.

> ➤ Part 5 contains two essays: *Erotica for Beginners* and *Shades of James - What Publishers Want,* both of which first appeared on Goodreads.com; and *The Body Stripped Bare*, a study of erotica in art and photography, first published in *The New Nude*.

> ➤ The Appendices list useful websites and a directory of erotic publishers.

Some writers are gifted. Most are not. The writers who become successful do so because they want it and work hard to get it. Writing is 10% inspiration, 90% perspiration.

Your vision of where you want to take your writing is the greatest asset you have. Without a destination, there is no journey. Once you have discovered the 'key' to EL James's success, the secret is not to press the key into hot wax and make a duplicate. On the contrary, you must study what is unique in her writing and seek out the uniqueness within your own.

PART 1

The Fifty Shades of Grey

Phenomena

First published in June 2011, *Fifty Shades of Grey* has sold more than 20 million copies worldwide and earned US-based British writer EL James upwards of $20 million. Her books have been translated into thirty languages and topped best-seller lists across the globe.

Film rights for *Fifty Shades of Grey* have been acquired by Universal Pictures for several million dollars and major stars are slated to play the leading roles of Anastasia Steele and Christian Grey.

Fifty Shades Darker and *Fifty Shades Freed*, books two and three in the Fifty Shades Trilogy, have likewise sold in their millions and two more pictures will be made to complete the series.

Fifty Shades of Grey is the first erotic book in modern times to find mainstream success and, in the UK, is the fastest-selling paperback ever. It has been described as 'mommy porn', due to its popularity among young moms and housewives, and is said to have captured the mood of the times.

Fetishes and erotic role play that would only a short time ago have been considered shocking or shameful have become accepted and embraced as healthy and totally normal, freeing women to explore their desires and sexuality. After almost half a century of 'female liberation', liberation in the bedroom (the kitchen counter, the back of the car, behind the mask) has come to pass.

In *Fifty Shades of Grey* the reader is introduced to the Red Room of Pain, a high-tech torture chamber. In this room, Anastasia learns to obey without question and submit to every kind of discipline. The first time Christian spanks Anastasia with his bare hand she accepts thirty good hard wallops on her backside and admits being aroused by the experience.

From spanking, Christian ratchets up the pain-pleasure principle through every variety of BDSM: bondage, discipline, sadism, masochism. Ana learns as she peels off her clothes that it is not just her naked body that is revealed but her deepest instincts, her subliminal desires. As she passes through the crumbling layers of her resistance, she discovers that in submission there is a form of domination and in the fiery bonfires of pain there is mysterious, unimagined pleasure.

This is the heart of erotica.

Even the cover designs of the three novels follow an erotic uptick. All in restrained shades of grey, *Fifty Shades* shows a man's knotted silver necktie; *Fifty Shades Darker* is illustrated with a striking costume mask; *Fifty Shades Freed* reaches the height of erotic tension with a pair of silver handcuffs.

What this says is, if you enjoyed book one, there's still a lot more to come in the sequels.

Christian dictates how Anastasia dresses, what she eats, how she should style her hair. At 'play', she addresses him as Sir, and knows if she fails to observe the rules she is 'contractually obligated' to obey, she will be punished. Having signed the 'pre-erotic' contract, Anastasia acquires a perverse freedom of choice. She can serve Christian like a slave girl, or break the rules knowing she will be spanked, cropped, whipped, paddled and suspended from the grid attached to the Red Room ceiling with its 'smell of leather, dark wood and sensuality'.

Why would she break the rules?

She knows the punishment will endow her 'inner goddess' (as Ana addresses her subconscious self) with an eruption of orgasms that take her to a state of ecstasy.

Detractors say this is demeaning, degrading, humiliating, without understanding that this is a crucial ingredient of the erotic interplay. Erotica is not about love and romance. Ana's submission to Christian's domination is designed to take them both to the peak of this often neglected aspect of our humanity: perfect union through perfect sex. Apart from all the obvious criteria, good relationships *are* about good sex.

At the beginning of the story, Anastasia is an uptight virgin, the product of a sexually-repressed society; a cipher, even, for the reactionary agenda. She moves so far beyond the pain pleasure frontier, when, three-quarters of the way through the novel, she whispers, 'Spank me, please,' Anastasia is riding on the crest of her erotic yearnings. The pain of being beaten will culminate in sexual congress that grants bliss for Ana, and allows Christian to attain a psychological and physical high. As Ana, and the reader, has already learned, due to a childhood trauma, Christian is unable to reach contentment in 'vanilla' sex. In Ana, he has found a partner capable of traveling with him through the clouds of externally imposed barriers to the mountain top of total sexual fulfillment. To this extent, he does not seek pleasure in domination and inflicting pain, but uses it to achieve perfection.

It is important to stress that the BDSM pursuits of Christian and Anastasia are consensual. She is safeguarded by the contract, and they have 'safety' words that apply the brakes if things go too far. This is different from the writing of the Marquis de Sade. The servant girls, prostitutes and society ladies flogged and violated in his work are not consenting and often under age. *Justine*, in his most famous novel, is only twelve. One of the rules imposed by erotic publishers in the United States and the United Kingdom is that participants are consenting and over the age of eighteen.

In EL James's three books, there is no abuse but an understanding between her two lead characters. She takes readers into the hearts and souls of Ana and Christian, while providing the landscape necessary to enrich the narrative and paint a complete picture of their life and times. A story with just two protagonists will lack tension if the reader is only invited to observe each character through the eyes of the other, or through inner discourse and reflection. Likewise, a story that races relentlessly from one sex scene to another is more likely to be pornographic than erotic, and deadly dull. EL James shrewdly gives her readers a palette of secondary characters and doesn't introduce sex, except as a romantic possibility, during the first third of *Fifty Shades of Grey*.

Was the sexual interlude at this critical point random?

No.

It was carefully chosen, as I will explain below.

All good stories, literary, mysteries, myths and legends, on the page and in film, pose a set of questions, doubts, dilemmas and goals. We turn the pages wondering if our heroes are ever going to overcome those problems and attain their goals. What the writer does is put obstacles in the way to make the journey more difficult. The reader's pleasure – and anxiety – comes from observing their heroes overcome, or fail to overcome, those obstacles. How they deal with problems defines character and allows the reader to identify, or not, with the people on the page.

Christopher Vogler in his seminal *The Writer's Journey* (Michael Wiese, 1998) says stories well up from a universal source in the shared unconscious and reflect universal concerns.

'They deal with childlike universal questions: Who am I? Where did I come from? Where will I go when I die? What is good and what is evil? What must I do about it? What will tomorrow be like? Where did yesterday go? Is there anybody else out there?'

The universal success of *Fifty Shades of Grey* grows from the writer asking and answering these universal questions. The questions are not spelt out, they are woven into the story's subtext, facets of character the reader witnesses in the way that Anastasia and Christian interact with each other, and the people and the world about them.

The Fifty Shades of Grey Phenomena

Playwrights in early Greek theater employed what was called *deus ex machina* to solve plot problem by introducing a new character or the miraculous intervention of God. The Marquis de Sade uses a similar device in *Justine*, where the ill-fated heroine confesses her debauched deeds to a stranger met at an inn. Anastasia would never be able to share her erotic escapades with her housemate, Kate Kavanagh. What EL James does is provide Anastasia with her 'inner goddess', an off-stage subconscious who subtly urges her to embrace this magical joyride.

Kate Kavanagh is sexy, outgoing and self-possessed, all the things Ana believes she isn't. Kate is Ana's opposite and mirror image; her adviser, her guilty-conscience, her 'mentor', as Vogler puts it, a vital personality in all great stories. In the student photographer José Luis Rodriguez, and Paul Clayton, the son of the owner of the shop where Ana works part-time, we have potential rivals and comparisons to Christian. Christian's family and employees form a sort of Greek chorus of secondary characters, their varying roles reflecting aspects of the two major characters and the human condition in its entirety.

To return the question above: Why did EL James save the first major erotic scene until she was one third of the way through her novel?

Plays traditionally and stories generally are divided into three acts. In movies, we may not be aware of this seamless segue from one to the other, but directors mark it by a moment of 'stasis', a stillness, a change of tempo and music, preparing us for the next part of the journey.

In the first act the characters are living in the 'normal' world where the reader gets to know their qualities, faults and foibles. Then something dramatic happens that turns the story in a new direction (in *Fifty Shades of Grey,* Ana has her bum tanned and likes it). In the second act, we observe Ana surmounting mainly self-imposed obstacles as she comes to terms with the fact that she enjoys life as a sex slave. This becomes the new 'normal' world, until Christian's erotic demands reach an extreme where Ana has doubts about the whole relationship and wants out, setting up the final act, the potential for compromise or a total split.

Master of the Universe

The *Fifty Shades* trilogy did not burst from EL James's pen like Old Faithful erupting in Jellystone Park. It materialized slowly, the shape of the story and the development of the characters growing with the writing. There was no *deus ex machina* standing in the wings. EL sat bent over her laptop and made it happen.

EL James has said she was inspired by Stephenie Meyer's Twilight Saga, *Twilight* and its sequels *New Moon, Eclipse and Breaking Dawn*. Originally, she borrowed the names of Meyer's characters, Edward Cullen and Bella Swan, and published stories on fantasy fiction websites under the title *Master of the Universe,* in honor, no doubt, of the epithet for those alpha males that roam the pages of Tom Wolfe's *Bonfire of the Vanities*. Using the extravagant pseudonym Snowqueens Icedragon, her *Master of the Universe* was criticized for its 'explicit' content and she removed it from the web.

Criticism is a sword with two edges. It can cut writers to pieces, or be the taste of cold steel that drives then to improve their writing, story-telling, characterization. Just as important, probably more important, is that criticism obliges writers to look at their work with fresh eyes – the eyes of the critic – to discover what it is the critics are banging on about. In EL James's case, it wasn't the writing, but the content. Her erotic imagery was too extreme for fantasy site readers. They, as critics, had spotted, probably without realizing it, what was in fact the original and distinctive quality of EL James's writing. She was experimenting with something new in that particular arena and people are suspicious of the new.

I have no idea if EL James ever considered abandoning her story and, along with 20 million others, am glad she didn't. What EL did was take a fresh look at her work. Instead of removing the erotic content from her manuscript, she enhanced it. She renamed her characters Anastasia Steele and

Christian Grey, devised three linked titles for what would become her trilogy, and launched her creation into a new and, as it turns out, waiting market.

Naming characters is just as important as finding the right title for your book.

The name's Bond – James Bond. You know by the ring of those hard consonants that this guy carries a license to kill and is going to save the world from despots. We can see images in our head the moment we hear mention of Scarlett O'Hara and Rhett Butler, Heathcliff, Philip Marlowe, Jay Gatsby, Sherlock Holmes, Holly Golightly, Harry Potter, Edward Cullen and Bella Swan. Vladimir Nabokov's unforgettable creation *Lolita* first drew breath in 1955 and the name remains synonymous with cute, sexually aware girls, as Romeo from Shakespeare's *Romeo and Juliet* is forever a lover and Scrooge, from Charles Dickens's *A Christmas Carol*, identifies a miser.

Anastasia Steele is another unforgettable creation. Steele defines flexibility and inner strength. Anastasia, apart from being a great name, is known historically as the youngest and prettiest daughter of Tsar Nicholas II of Russia, executed by the communists in 1918. While the graves of the other members of the royal family have been found, Anastasia's never was, fuelling rumors that she escaped and giving the name henceforth the illusive, mysterious quality ideal for fiction. Ana, the shortened version used interchangeably in the book, balances the extravagance of Anastasia and has a feel of modesty and reliability, inner qualities of the character.

Christian Grey is a more complex creation. The name Christian, particularity in the United States, where the trilogy is set, tells us the man is an all-American with values we associate with the nation – integrity, independence, get up and go. Grey is the color of his eyes (that 'glitter with promise') and denotes his grey areas, of which there are many. In the childhood ordeal Christian experienced, the writer sets up his kinky sexuality. As Anastasia notes, he's 'fifty shades of fucked up'.

With Anastasia and Christian in place, EL divided her work into three parts to create what would become the trilogy.

Before the book saw print, *Fifty Shades of Grey* appeared in May 2011 as an ebook with The Writers' Coffee Shop, based in Australia. Six months later, in September 2011, *Fifty Shades Darker* was released and, in January 2012, *Fifty Shades Freed*. The small, back-room publishing house had a zero advertizing budget and set about promoting EL through viral PR and social networking sites. Sales began to mount through the best marketing machine known to man: word-of-mouth. The success of the trilogy has a deeper more lustrous gloss in that it grew from humble beginnings, a sign that if the product is right, it will find a market.

EL James had taken note of the original criticism, but stuck to her guns. She wrote the books she wanted to write, the story that inspired her and she believed in, not teenager fantasy, but full-blown female erotica. She had astutely decided to write three books, which has proven to be the best way to break through in internet publishing. Readers may once have been willing to wait a year or two for the next novel by their favorite author. The digital age is instant. If a book touches the public mood, you must follow it up straight away or you lose the momentum. EL James had covered every base.

It says above 'she wrote the books she wanted to write.' This is essential, a golden rule. There is no artistic pursuit, few life pursuits, as tough as staring at a screen, a typewriter, a blank sheet of paper and putting black on white. We have all seen that scene in the movies where the writer – in beaten up clothes in a dimly-lit room – sits over a lined pad scribbling a sentence, then screwing the sheet up and throwing it in the bin across the room where hundreds of paper balls litter the floor. This isn't a screenwriter fantasy. This is the screenwriter's life. The writer's life.

Writers will tell you they would rather clean the kitchen floor than write. They are not joking. When you clean the kitchen floor, you start with a dirty floor and end with a clean floor. There is a beginning, middle and end. Something has been completed and achieved. All stories take characters on a journey from one state to a new, often opposite state. The bully becomes the savior. The spurned lover gets the girl.

James Bond saves the world. Prudish Anastasia gets kinky. The floor gets clean.

Writers set off on this journey with their characters because they are driven. It's an itch they can't scratch. The monkey on their back. They write because they have to write. The fact that it tires you physically and drains you mentally makes it an absolute imperative that you love your characters, the evil as well as the saintly, know the genre inside out and write what moves you, what drives you, what you are compelled to share with others. If you are just a hack jumping on the band wagon trying to create a bogus best-seller, you won't hit the charts, you're more likely to fail and hit the bottle.

You must love your characters? Yes, like your own newborn. Christen them with a name that *feels* right for their temperament (or runs contrary to it), a name that sounds right when you see their image in your mind and read *what they have to say when it emerges on the page* – and yes, once they are fleshed out, *they* will say what *they* want to say and *do* what they want to *do*. Characters are your children. Once they are old enough – before the crucial one-third in turning point – there will be endless fights as they make their journey. Character drives story and the characters are in the driving seat.

Give characters a specific age, physiognomy, place of birth, education, family background, ambitions, interests. Give them a quirk. He's a lawyer and secret drag racer. She's a first grade teaches who adores lesbian leather clubs. Think about their height and weight. You don't have to spell it out: Bob was as broad as a rowing boat and stood 6' 4" in his socks. Show the reader he's tall when Wendy can't reach the pasta pot on the top shelf and Bob takes it down without stretching his arm. Give your characters a birth sign: is she a vague but compassionate Pisces, he a generous but dogmatic Leo. Are they water and fire, she dousing his flames, he making her erupt in steam; or air and fire, usually in harmony. Whether astrology grabs you or not, it is a useful tool for fashioning personality traits, and most writers keep a copy of *Star Signs* on their bookshelf alongside *Naming Your Baby*.

Star signs, physical attributes, biographies and the objectives of your characters are the skeleton of your story. This information doesn't have to be spelled out on the page, but knowing every intimate detail of your creations blows air into their lungs. Sometimes, writers get to know their characters so well they end up meeting them and putting themselves in the story, a common device employed wittily by Martin Amis in his novel *Money*.

Once you've filled a notepad with background material and written the first draft, like EL James after abandoning *Master of the Universe,* you will then have to go back through those thousands of words editing what you have written. If there are three rules for writers: READ, READ, READ, there are three rules for the rewriting stage: EDIT, EDIT, EDIT. Those million of dollars don't come falling out of the sky like the frogs in Paul Thomas Anderson's inventive *Magnolia*. Writing is hard work. In fact, there is a useful website called www.writingishardwork.com with loads of insider tips.

Writingishardwork advises completing the entire manuscript before going back to edit. This may suit some writers, but it is not a hard rule. If editing as you go feels right, it is right. The goal is to finish the manuscript, not that a manuscript ever seems truly finished. After two edits you'll feel inclined to take on a third and fourth. But the time comes when you have to type *the end* and send the baby off into the market, setting off another cycle of author angst. It is said that publishing a book is like giving birth and, when it's finally out there, writers suffer postpartum blues. They get over it when a new idea grabs them and the toil and the backache start all over again.

One downside of the editing phase is that writers sometimes polish their work until it shines so brightly readers are blinded by the sheer brilliance. In writing, as in life, it is finding the right balance. When you have found that balance, and are satisfied with your work, that's not the time to send it off; manuscripts sent out too hastily come back even quicker. Instead, the typescript should be put aside for at least a week and, when you take it out again, you are more likely to see the clichés, repetitions, the pretentious, the need to change the obtuse to the simple. We rarely use verbose phrases when we speak, so don't let the long-winded and pompous to creep into your writing.

Can you change a long sentence into two short sentences by taking out an and or a but? Shorter sentences read quicker and feel more compelling. Is there a sub-clause that adds nothing? Have you used a long word that can be substituted by a short one; a foreign phrase that could be replaced by words in English?

To say that all writing is re-writing is an absolute truism, now more than ever. Few publishers in these austere times employ full-time editors. Good projects are often rejected because of minor errors in editing, grammar and construction. And digital self-published authors will be mocked and criticized if their work falls below an acceptable professional standard.

Whatever goes down on paper, however well it looks on the page or sounds when you read it aloud, that first gush of words is unlikely to produce anything of great merit. What that first gush will do is give you something to work with; it is the map of the journey, not the journey; the clay, not the Ming vase. The plot for a good story in tandem with sincere feelings and the desire to create are not sufficient to produce good writing. Nor is first impression, stream of consciousness writing that sounds lyrical as it comes gushing from the top of your head, but simply will not grip an audience without a solid backbone supporting a healthy skeleton.

That old scoundrel and genius Oscar Wilde said once: 'I was working on the proof of one of my poems all the morning, and took out a comma. In the afternoon I put it back again.'

Excessive? Not at all. If writing has one secret it is rewriting. You must learn how to let go, take out the glitter, kill your darlings, as William Faulkner put it. There is no easy way to rewrite. It is self-taught. It requires discipline and labor.

On a brighter note, early drafts with their corrections and coffee rings always look and sound as if there is still endless room for improvement. Once the hand-written notes have gone and the pages are neatly aligned, what is left miraculously reads better than it ever did in the early stages of the creation. It is not the end of the journey but the end is in sight.

I will add a second quote from Oscar Wilde: 'A man can be happy with any woman as long as he does not love her.' This has been true of the erotic genre for generations. EL James has broken the mold.

Banning Books

Why Shades of Grey took off so fast and has traveled so far has consumed tens of thousands of column inches in the world press and countless hours of discussion in the media. The largest segment of the reader demographic is women over thirty, usually with young children, thus the ill-named 'mommy porn', who were able to enjoy this guilty pleasure devouring the pages electronically, that is privately, on devices such as tablets, Kindle, the Barnes & Noble Nook. For those who bought the pocket book, the publishers veiled the material in subtlety, hinting at the explicit content rather than screaming it. In a pornographic age where every shoe ad features a pair of mouth-watering breasts, this was a stroke of genius.

The ultimate accolade for *Fifty Shades of Grey*, the subliminal dream of all writers, came in March 2012, when the Florida County Library removed copies of the book due to its 'overt sexual content'. There's nothing like banning a book to make it hot and that's exactly what happened. So many people protested, librarians took the books out of storage and put them back on the shelves.

Since the launch of the trilogy at the beginning of 2012, 'erotic writers have noticed a welcome spike in sales,' according to a spokesman at Xcite Books. Erotica is in. Not that it's ever been out.

Defining Erotic

- Is there a simple guide for writing the next great erotic novel?

- **No**

- Is there a blueprint, a formula, a paradigm, a checklist?

- **No**

- Are there explicit rules?

- **Sort of. Maybe. But not exactly.**

I will repeat three words of advice for those who want to be the next famous – or infamous – erotic novelist:

- **READ**

- **READ**

- **READ**

We will come back to tips on writing the next great novel, and exactly why *Fifty Shades of Grey* hit the heights.

But the first rule of writing is reading.

There are scores, hundreds, thousands of websites where you can download FREE erotic/porn novels and short stories.

That *isn't* the best place to start.

There is a lot of trash out there, quickly-written, poorly edited, cliché-ridden knock-offs. This will not help the new writer. It will do more harm than good.

EL James is a phenomena. The Marquis de Sade is a legend. But there are many other great writers whose books should be on your shelf before you put fingers to keyboards. The list is random and includes heterosexual erotica, gay and lesbian.

Anaïs Nin

- *A Spy in the House of Love*
- *House of Incest*
- *Under a Glass Bell*
- *Delta of Venus*
- *Seduction of the Minotaur*

Catherine Millet

- *The Sexual Life of Catherine M.*
- *Jealousy: The Other Life of Catherine M.*

Melissa Panarello

- *One Hundred Strokes of the Brush Before Bed*
- *The Scent of Your Breath*
- *In the Name of Love*

Pauline Réage (Anne Desclos)

- *The Story of O*

Anne Rice (as A. N. Roquelaure): *The Sleeping Beauty Trilogy*

- *The Claiming of Sleeping Beauty*
- *Beauty's Punishment*
- *Beauty's Release*

Alan Hollinghurst

- *The Folding Star*

Sarah Waters

- *Tipping The Velvet*
- *Affinity*
- *Fingersmith*

Rita Mae Brown

* *Rubyfruit Jungle*

Jeanette Winterson

* *Oranges Are Not The Only Fruit*

* *Written on the Body*

Georges Bataille

* *Story of the Eye*

Georges Bataille's *Story of the Eye* is his only erotic novel (it was made into a film in 2004) and the writer is better known as the author of *Eroticism*, a study of taboo and transgression – (Marion Boyers Publishers, 2006). Bataille describes eroticism thus:

> Eroticism is assenting to life up to the point of death. Strictly speaking, this is not a definition, but I think the formula gives the meaning of eroticism better than any other.

Assenting to life *to the point of death* is accepting all possibilities and extremes, and taking them to a point where ecstasy is at such a fever pitch that even death would be an acceptable culmination of the pleasure.

This is an extreme few people seek in life, but erotic literature isn't a reality show. It is not a carbon copy of life. It is a fantasy, a way to give readers a glimpse of another world, an alternative universe, much as Stephenie Meyer has done with her cast of vampires and werewolves, and George Lucus with the *Star Wars* films.

Bataille explains erotica as an 'exuberance of life', a psychological quest 'not alien to death.' He adds a quote from de Sade: 'There is no better way to know death than to link it with some licentious image.' The French call orgasm *la* petite mort, the little death that announces, not the height of pleasure but pleasure's end. Orgasm – particularly for men – brings sexual elation to its termination, a metaphorical demise at the very moment of perfection.

23

In de Sade, we find damsels tethered in dungeons; Anaïs Nin's whipping sessions take place in the sinister House of Incest; Anastasia is shackled with black leather cuffs to the grid on the ceiling in the Red Room of Pain, what Christian alternatively calls the 'playroom'. In each case, heroines face the risk of torture knowing that, while death is at one extreme of the chastisement, rapture lies at the other. The erotic, on the page and in life, is about exploring our sexuality, extending the bliss, delving into the dark heart of desire.

This, from a literary perspective, poses two questions: what is erotic, and what is the difference between erotic and pornographic?

There is more than one answer. My first suggestion, simpler than that of Georges Bataille, is that an erotic story is told from the point of view of the female, while the pornographic is the visions and fantasies of the male. There are exceptions, but that's a suitable first principle.

The erotic captures a sensual, unforeseen, ambiguous situation. A woman sitting at the bar showing three inches of bare leg above black stockings is more erotic than, say, a guy clutching his quivering member prior to lancing the defenseless female. A description or an image of a woman masked in a maid's uniform, or high heels and suspenders, or gagged and handcuffed, will almost certainly be more interesting, menacing, more transgressive than a pouting nude with spread legs and heaving bosoms. *Ooo, it's so big I'm frightened.*

Erotica is the creation of mysterious or unexpected or forbidden circumstances and situations. The erotic is not romantic, rarely tender or particularly emotional. When a man in our story spots the woman revealing her stocking tops in the bar, he will not drop down on the stool beside her and say 'Hi, honey, can you pass the nuts?' That's banal, possibly the beginnings of something romantic, or comic, or ironic. It is not erotic.

The man in tune with the erotic charge created by the woman's disregard for acceptable public behavior may say: I have a car outside. I want you to follow me out of the bar and get into the back. Do not ask any questions.

Now what?

This is fiction. Anything can happen. What we have established is that the man is not looking for a romantic interlude. If the woman is tuned to the same erotic pulse, neither is she. What happens next can follow any path that comes to mind. One trick used by fiction writers is to ask themselves: what is the most unlikely thing that can happen, and that's what they run with.

The erotic is a subtle interaction, a game, generally played between a man and woman. The convention makes the man dominant (Christian Grey), while the woman is submissive (Anastasia), although, again, the roles can be reversed. Same sex erotica follows the same rules and breaks the same rules. The very essence of the erotic is breaking rules. To write erotica, you must first learn the rules, the conventions, in order to know how to bend and break them.

For some, the difference between erotica and pornography is merely semantic. 'Tabloid babe reveals all' can be seen as a bit of harmless fun or, by contrast, a symbol of the pornification of society: trainer bras for seven year olds, C-list celebrities 'getting their tits out'. Fashion doesn't dress the female, it undresses her. Nudity is a fetish. There are websites devoted entirely to showing girls walking naked through crowded parks and city streets. There are websites showing every known kink and fetish ever imagined, women portrayed as objects of male fantasy, perpetuating the masquerade of femininity as vane, trivial and passive.

This is fertile soil for porn, soft-core or hard-core, to use the jargon, storytellers typically showing men as burly hunters and women as timid bunnies or pussies or ponies, weak insipid playthings who secretly crave 'a good seeing to.' Male viewpoint accounts of sexual encounters are often about 'capturing' or 'confining' or 'subduing' the female, as if the female is wildlife and sex is a gladiatorial sport. Descriptions of male attitudes, hungers and needs are often clumsy and barbaric. Pornography stimulates sexual craving. The erotic captures the sensual, the inexplicable, the exotic.

A woman entering the erotic arena doesn't parade herself naked. She reveals a bare back or shoulders, or her toes and tattoos in a way that creates desire not through what's on show, but what's hidden. She is a riddle to be unraveled. She is not prey being hunted, but another hunter, a woman aware of her own cravings who seeks a partner who understands them; or, alternatively, she is a woman unaware of her subliminal longings who grows aware through the 'mentoring' of a lover. The relationship will inspire a more complex plot and a requires a more finely-tuned style of writing.

The differences in form can be seen as a question of class: high-brow versus low brow. Or, on a base level, art as opposed to commerce: porn written solely to excite the senses and rattle the tills, erotica being a literary endeavor that holds a mirror to society through a strong storyline, subtext, believable characters and the sexual content arising out of plot. In the introduction to the anthology *Totally Heterotica*, Susie Bright puts it like this: 'The very word *erotic* implies superior value, fine art, an aesthetic which elevates the mind and incidentally stimulates the body'.

The erotic/porn debate is not confined to the US and Europe. In a *Times of India* article, Jug Suraiya describes pornography as a form of exploitation representing an impoverishment of our sexual imagination. 'Pornography is a dumbed-down diagram leading to a cul-de-sac whose only destination is libidinal claustrophobia,' he writes. 'Erotica represents the complex cartography of desire, full of hazard and mystery, inviting endless exploration.'

Violet Blue, author of *The Smart Girl's Guide to Porn*, describing porn and erotica in film, puts it like this: 'Porn is something that is a graphic sexual image that conjures up an animalistic reaction in you. You like it or you don't.' She adds. 'Erotica also is graphic sexual imagery, but it has an extra component or several extra components that resonate with the viewer, be it artistic, be it passionate, be it something that emotionally engages you, be it something that parlays into a fantasy that you have about sexuality or the way that you relate to the people on the screen.'

Sex scenes in contemporary movies have become ever more explicit and are largely portrayed in a romantic context. Among the notable exceptions are the violently sexual *Irreversible,* directed by Gaspar Noé and starring Monica Bellucci, and *American Psycho,* directed by Marry Harron, with Christian Bale. Stanley Kubrick tried his hand at erotica with Tom Cruise and Nicole Kidman in *Eyes Wide Shut,* the story of a man who sets out on a long night of sexual discovery, without ever discovering very much. A film more sleazy and comedic, in spite of the title, is John Bacchus's *Erotic Survivor,* a spoof on the CBS TV show, *Survivor,* with, among other things, naked contestants cutting through the jungle with a giant dildo.

To make a clear distinction in the porn/erotic divide, we have to go back to the 1970s and compare Luis Buñuel's *That Obscure Object of Desire* (1977) with Gerard Damian's 'porn chic' *Deep Throat* (1972). In *Deep Throat,* Linda Lovelace (playing herself) learns that her clitoris is in her throat and she can only achieve orgasm through oral sex, a contrivance that sets up an obvious succession of titivating scenes. Buñuel tells the story of a middle-aged man obsessed with a young woman who taunts him, even sleeps with him, but never allows him to enter that obscure object of desire. His film engages us with an erotic promise and inspires questions about aging, loyalty, beauty and how men and women each view sex in a different light, a premise of less consequence today, but still relevant.

What have movies got to do with erotic literature? EL James's books are being turned into movies. If the films score at the box office, Hollywood will be scanning the titles in search of product.

Show Don't Tell

Fifty Shades of Grey is Anastasia's story. She tells it from her viewpoint and she is the character who goes through major life changes. From a virgin without a boyfriend she metamorphoses into a sexual submissive dating a wealthy master of erotica. From a self-doubting student with twitches and bitten lips, she becomes the ultimate object of desire.

The way EL James hooks her readers is to 'show' us those changes without undue author intrusion. She doesn't 'tell' us Ana is attractive. On the contrary, Ana believes she is plain with bad hair and a total disaster when it comes to choosing clothes. Her worldly housemate Kate Kavanagh doesn't share that opinion. Neither do her friends José Luis or Paul Clayton. By showing us that boys are interested in Ana, we learn that she's attractive without being force fed the information. And we like her more for her modesty.

We know Christian is handsome, not because the author tells us, but through Ana, whose opinion we grow to trust. We discover details of his life and business from third party disclosures, and EL uses dialogue to add to the information. When two people discuss a mutual friend, there is a sense of immediacy. The reader 'shares' the secret, while the author provides back story without listing details like a cop's suspect report. The way Christian Grey handles machines, people and circumstances show us what sort of man he is through action, and we learn more about Ana through her reactions, inner thoughts and feelings.

Scenes describing action require more time and space; the three *Shades of Grey* books check in at almost 1600 pages, and there are occasions when a short cut is conveniently employed to move the plot along like a bridge spanning the gaps between the drama; a moment to pause and take breath. Describing a room or building is simple and in some books have the ring of real estate blurbs. With Ana, we have a guide who marvels at each new discovery and we see everything through her eyes.

Drawing on what Ana sees is valuable, but only uses one of the senses. We learn more about Christian, and Ana, when she describes the *smell* of wax and leather; the *sound* of the cane cutting the still air; the *taste* on her tongue when she licks Christian's damp skin; the *feel* of his hand striking her ass and the fiery bloom of her own flesh after a thrashing. Hearing, sight, smell, taste and touch. The five senses are wonderful things and should be laid out on the writer's desk ready to be picked up at any time.

You need adjectives and adverbs in descriptions, but they should be used sparingly and selected as if you are laying a mosaic one small chip of stone at a time. Generally speaking, the word 'very' is almost never useful; if a man's tall he's tall, if the music's loud it's loud. If a beating leaves welts that burn, it isn't very painful, it's agony.

There are books and websites galore with info on show don't tell. Here's my own simple rule:

- She was sad = TELL
- She wept = SHOW

To broaden the illustration and return to the bar scene, here are two examples; you know which is which:

- The girl was to die for. When she crossed the bar in her red dress and sky high heels the men couldn't take their eyes off her.

- Conversations stilled and you could hear the tap of the woman's heels as she glided across the bar. Her arms were pale in a sleeveless black dress and every woman in the place was listening as she ordered a vodka tonic.

Henry Miller, author of the quasi-erotic *Tropic of Cancer* and *Tropic of Capricorn,* wrote 11 Commandments for Writers:

1. Work on one thing at a time until finished.
2. Start no more new books, add no more new material to *Black Spring* (his autobiographical novel).
3. Don't be nervous. Work calmly, joyously, recklessly on whatever is in hand.
4. Work according to Program and not according to mood. Stop at the appointed time!
5. When you can't create you can work.

6. Cement a little every day, rather than add new fertilizers.
7. Keep human! See people, go places, drink if you feel like it.
8. Don't be a drought-horse! Work with pleasure only.
9. Discard the Program when you feel like it — but go back to it the next day.
10. Concentrate. Narrow down. Exclude.
11. Forget the books you want to write. Think only of the book you are writing.
    Write first and always. Painting, music, friends, cinema, all these come afterwards.

To make it 12 Commandments, here is some advice from George Orwell: Never use a metaphor, simile or other figure of speech which you are used to seeing in print. The example above, 'to die for' makes the point.

Good Writing

The word erotic comes from the Greek word eros, meaning desire. According to Wikipedia, it is 'generally understood to refer to a state of sexual arousal or anticipation of such, an insistent sexual impulse, desire, or pattern of thoughts, as well as a philosophical contemplation concerning the aesthetics of sexual desire, sensuality and romantic love.'

Wiki describes pornography or porn as the 'explicit portrayal of sexual subject matter...involving the depiction of acts in a sensational manner, with the entire focus on the physical act, so as to arouse quick intense reactions'.

The erotic has depth. Porn doesn't. The erotic creates *an insistent sexual impulse, desire, or pattern of thoughts, as well as a philosophical contemplation concerning the aesthetics of sexual desire*. The difference, then, between porn and the erotic is good writing.

Good writing is the creation of memorable characters that you love and you must convey that feeling to your readers. Your creations must be 'real' with qualities and flaws: they lose things, make mistakes, they are kind and stubborn, vane and modest, they have affairs, and get caught. In an erotic novel, in all good literature, the leading players are at the point of making changes in their lives and are about to do something rebellious, impulsive or crazy, something they have never done before. Reader pleasure comes from joining your characters in the adventure and traveling with them.

An erotic novel needs turning points, pauses, changes of pace, as do all novels, but more so. A book with non-stop groping and grunting quickly grows tiresome. Pleasure to remain pleasurable must be constantly nourished and renewed. To enhance that pleasure, an erotic novel must surprise readers with unexpected meetings, situations and couplings that turn the story in a new direction and move your characters towards an ever greater understanding of their goals, needs and desires. They will have doubts. The reader must *see* their doubts, and we must be with them when they set out on their journey into that forbidden, often unfamiliar realm of the erotic.

Anything forbidden and mysterious is immediately attractive. Like a moth moving closer to the flame, we are drawn to those things which frighten us. The reader of erotica wants to savor the fear, be scorched by the flame, if only from the distance of the written word. In the wake of EL James's books, the erotic bar has been set higher, but the same intrinsic literary rules apply: sexual content must never be contrived. It must evolve through plot and should arouse both physically and mentally. Good erotic writing allows you to suspend disbelief and believe.

The Secret

This is the plot of EL James's novel *Fifty Shades of Grey*.

> Anastasia Steele is a literature student with 'bad hair' she wears in a pony tail. She is modest in manner, makeup and dress, an inexperienced virgin, the opposite of her confident housemate, Kate. When Kate convinces the 'enigmatic' tycoon Christian Grey to accept an interview

with the student newspaper, she goes down with flu and Ana agrees to go in her place.

There is an immediate sexual tension between Ana and Christian. Ana surprises herself that she is attracted to this rich, confident, manipulative 'adonis'. He can't believe he is attracted to Ana, a gauche, innocent girl. He sets out to secretly meet her again and the attraction between them grows.

When the prospect of sex enters the relationship, Anastasia dreams of storybook romance and is shocked to learn that Christian suffers 'inner demons' that inflame unacceptable desires involving domination and submission, bondage and corporal punishment. Her first instinct is to escape, but she is falling in love with Christian and wants to understand the reason why he cannot love her in the 'normal' way.

Christian promises to reveal those reasons if Ana agrees to sign a contract that outlines the erotic activities he wants them to share. Ana negotiates the terms of the contract and accepts a get-out clause that allows her to null the agreement at any time. Christian makes it all seem so reasonable, she accepts the terms and sets off on a sexual rollercoaster ride that takes her to the heights of ecstasy and changes her life forever.

So far, so conventional. But what EL James has done that's different is to take the romance genre and make it erotic. She has not taken the erotic and added romance. This may seem like splitting hairs, but there is a subtle difference that emerges in the writing and sustains the dynamic tension. cliffo

The erotic traditionally is light on tenderness and emotions. EL's books are deeply tender, strikingly emotional, with all the disappointments and tears, the promise and heartache of true love. We feel for Ana with her lack of self-confidence, lip-biting and tics. But what EL James has succeeded in doing is make her readers feel for Christian as well.

Christian is described on Page 1 of her 500 page first novel as enigmatic, and unhurriedly allows the enigmas and mysteries to surface. EL makes him devilishly handsome, not merely a millionaire, but a billionaire, with a 'state-of-the-art' pad and boy toys that whizz Ana and the reader off in fast cars and a helicopter Christian flies himself. It is the American Dream redrawn for the erotic.

Anastasia wants to lick Christian's soft skin, taste him, feel him deep inside her, yearnings described from Ana's point of view. EL James reveals Christian's longings through intimate emails and a form of dialogue characteristic of romance and rare in erotic literature. These exchanges allow us to catch our breath as we wait for the next wave of violent passion to seize us in its grip. The erotic scenes – in which her best writing emerges – are not incidental, as in romance, they are the heart and soul of the book.

Thanks to EL James, the erotic has come of age. There's a hunger for stories that take readers to places where no one has been before, a universe where the fever of sex is portrayed in fresh, lyrical ways. The erotic craves originality, innovation, a fresh eye. It demands insightful descriptions, inventive similes, unpredictable plotlines. Of all the literary genres, it is the only one where there's always a welcome mat for new writers.

PART 2

The Life of the Marquis de Sade

The Marquis de Sade is the most renowned erotic writer of all time. He spent almost half his sixty-four years in various prisons, including the Bastille, and was finally sent to an insane asylum where he wrote his most famous works, *Justine* and *120 Days of Sodom*, the pages of which were smuggled out a folio at a time, printed and sold in secret to an insatiable readership. Banned, burned, censored and condemned, there has always been a huge market for erotica.

Donatien Alphonse François (1740 – 1814) was the son of Comte Jean-Baptiste François Joseph de Sade and Marie-Eléonore de Maillé, the Lady-in-Waiting to the Princess of Condé. De Sade's parents resided at the House of Condé, the 16th century palace where their son grew up and which would become the fictionalized setting for much of his later writing: the Gothic chambers connected by candlelit corridors, grim stairways and shadowy dungeons nurturing his macabre imagination and planting the seeds of the literary genre he took to new extremes.

After studying with his uncle, the Abbé de Sade, he was sent to the Jesuit school before pursuing a military career. He fought in the Seven Years' War (1756 – 1763), the hostilities stemming from the colonial ambitions of the great powers: Britain, Portugal, Russia, the Prussian Hohenzollerns, the Archdukes of Austria, the Holy Roman Emperors and the Spanish and French Bourbons.

At barely sixteen, in June 1756, de Sade's baptism of fire took place when the armies of the Maréchal de Richelieu stormed Port-Mahon. Wearing a scarlet uniform with a plumed helmet, de Sade was in the vanguard of the attack.

Following 'fierce and murderous combat,' with a lone companion he secured an enemy stronghold and his bravery was 'mentioned in dispatches,' according to Gilbert Lêly, de Sade's biographer. De Sade would later write that during the skirmish 'his soul was on fire.' He saw death all around and felt no compassion bathing his sword in the blood of those enemy soldiers who stood in his way. He was swiftly promoted and led a company of Dragoons the following year during France's assault on the Rhine.

The Seven Years' War was the first conflict to have global impact. Battles were fought across Europe, parts of Africa, India, the Philippines, Canada and the United States. Not since the Crusades had warfare been so bloodthirsty and merciless. More than a million people were slaughtered. Entire cities were pillaged and demolished; entire populations put to the sword.

It was in this furnace of carnage and misery where de Sade's soul was forged and the map of his future began to form. Climbing the ranks to Colonel, his diary through those years changed from heroic accounts of battles won and soldiers meeting death in a noble cause, to a mocking criticism of the military high command, the corruption and duplicity at the heart of government, all government, and the futility of war.

He had seen with his own eyes massacres blessed by the Holy Roman Church and torture executed in the name of the Crown. He came to view the ethics of his times, and of life itself, as hollow, hypocritical and meaningless, a grand lie perpetrated by Church and State. The only way to endure this absurdity, he reasoned, was to live in freedom without value judgments, religion or morality. He saw all existence as a struggle between master and slave, predator and prey, and determined to enjoy his own good fortune as one of the hunters.

Arriving back in Paris a war hero, de Sade began to put his theories into practice. Within months, several street walkers had protested to the Police Commissioner over his 'unmentionable' acts, whipping, bondage, torture, the panoply of perversions and brutality he had witnessed in the wake of battle and would later appear in gory relish on the pages of his books. Put under surveillance, detectives wrote reports on his vile deeds, lingering in imitation of de Sade over each 'sordid' act with lurid descriptions that survive to this day in the archives of Provence.

The drawing dates to 1760, when the Sade was nearly 20 years old. It's the only known authentic portrait of the Marquis.

After spending a few nights of reflection in the jailhouse, de Sade realized that his pleasures were going to cost him a great deal more than he could afford on his army pension and family allowance. Tall, good-looking, if ravaged, he courted and quickly married the heiress Renée-Pélagie de Montreuil, the daughter of a magistrate. They made their home at the castle above Lacoste, a spectacular hill town overlooking the Provence countryside; today, the restored edifice a place of pilgrimage for admirers of de Sade's writing, philosophy and, no doubt, his lifestyle.

De Sade constructed a theatre within the castle walls and the plays written by an 'anonymous' author began to acquire loyal patronage by the time his father died in 1767, when he assumed the title, Marquis. The productions were bizarre, as well as blasphemous, in that, while the performers portrayed perverse and vicious acts, they discussed wide-raging political, religious and philosophical issues. The more prurient the work, the more the men of Lacoste clamored for tickets, if only to condemn with first hand knowledge their crude and salacious content.

The Marquis watched the audiences watching his work and came to believe that in the soul of those bourgeois tradesmen was a streak of sadism – the word invented in honor of his name, albeit after his lifetime, and linked forever with masochism, that strand of the human psyche he saw in the souls of the weak who, in turn, had every potential to grab the whip-handle if and when the chance arose. Like the Chinese symbols *yin* and *yang*, each has the seed of the opposite within, and each requires the other to be complete.

Sex is the fundamental driving force of our species; of all species. What de Sade recognized was that sex of reproduction, 'vanilla' sex as it would become known in erotic literature, was disappointing and inspired banal, tedious prose. The *Literary Review's* Bad Sex Awards have become an annual event for bibliophiles, the novelists in contention ambivalent about appearing on the list and having their metaphor-laden scribblings read out to a bemused public on the radio.

Had de Sade been writing today, he would never have suffered such humiliation. He identified the line between a love story and an erotic story and recognized that, the further that line was crossed, the greater the potential for creating compulsive narratives. He was conscious of his own erotic nature and, as he watched the burgers of Lacoste glued to their seats in his theatre, he became aware that aspects of that nature existed in every man – and woman. While a handful of prostitutes reported his depraved deeds, just as many did not.

He discerned from this that his companions on his erotic journey would have different levels of tolerance and, more important, that tolerance to pain both increases and reaches a point when pain becomes pleasure.

This was particularly important when it comes to writing erotica. Stories need this racking up of tension and intensification to keep readers interested. The maiden who faints after six lashes from a bull-whip will learn to accept a dozen. The serving girl kept naked among guests at dinner will, in the erotic context, find pleasure walking naked through the city streets. People, once they have overcome the cultural inhibitions, enjoy their nudity. Concealment is a subliminal revelation; as essayist John Langdon-Davies put it: 'It is quite certain that Adam assumed the fig leaf, not in order to hide his shame, but in order to draw attention to something of which he was proud.'

Nudity, bondage, corporal punishment, multiple partners, slavery, every form of role play with can imagine today has always been with us. Erotic composition survives from the first Chinese dynasty. From Ancient Greece we have an infinite collection of erotic verse including the work of the first 'lesbian' writer, Sappho of Lesbos, who died around 570 BC. The great Roman thinker, Ovid, dabbled in the erotic, as did Shakespeare, better known for his love elegy *Romeo and Juliet*, he also turned his quill to the sensuous poems *Venus and Adonis* and *The Rape of Lucrece*. The above mentioned works are included in Derek Parker's excellent 1980 study *An Anthology of Erotic Verse*.

The *Kama Sutra* first appeared 2000 years ago and rivals the Bible and the Koran as one of the best known books of all time. In mediaeval India, the Sanskrit poet Kokkoka wrote *Secrets of Love*, a new manual of sexual positions for King Venudutta. The 17th century novel, *The Carnal Prayer Mat*, by Chinese author Li Yu, was the *Shades of Grey* of its time and became a hot best-seller. Look for a pot-boiler published five years ago and it has probably disappeared from the bookshops, but trawl the internet and you will find most of the works mentioned in these pages.

The Fifty Shades of Grey Phenomena

In more recent times, erotic writers from Anaïs Nin to E. L. James, have continued to reshape the genre, while sticking closely to the blueprint set down by the Marquis de Sade: submissive females are drawn to dominant males (soldiers, aristocrats game keepers, clergy) and discover sensual pleasure through acts involving restraints, gagging, punishment by hand, whip, strap and cane; humiliation, including being kept as a slave, being urinated and defecated on; the combinations of these acts now commonly united under the heading BDSM, a universal abbreviation for bondage and discipline (BD), dominance and submission (DS), sadism and masochism (SM). BDSM is described by the Urban Dictionary as: 'A physical, psychological and usually sexual power-role-play with consensual participants.'

The consensual aspect of BDSM is the principle difference between contemporary erotic literature and that pioneered by the Marquis de Sade. His stories are decadent and nihilistic with pitiless protagonists and simpering heroines stripped of their morality, dignity and clothes. No pornographic or erotic writing since has matched the power of his pen – nor the breadth of his research.

The Marquis de Sade grasped the first rule of the budding author: write about what you know about. As a young man growing up in the House of Condé, he would have seen churchmen and aristocrats seducing young virgins and house maids below his very roof. Added to his experiences on the battlefield slaughtering men with lance and sword was his careful study of human psychology. He didn't only whip and unite in coitus with the prostitutes he procured, he observed their reactions and lusts, their greed and hypocrisy. The same with the townsmen of Lacoste. They condemned each barrier being torn down and, in secret, many imitated the Marquis and followed the same path of excess and debauchery.

When his wife's sister, Anne-Prospère, moved to live at the castle, he seduced her and made her partner in his clandestine orgies. Servants, of both sexes, he saw as fair game. His writing became more depraved, as did his life, which he led with what he called 'extreme freedom,' and what the existentialists more than a century later would call 'authenticity.' In Provence, he felt safe from the prying eyes of the capital and, something often forgotten, while his literature became more transgressive, so, too, did his political writing, which he pursued with almost as much fervor and which would, perversely, save his life.

De Sade's wife gave birth to three children, two sons and a daughter, while he maintained relations with her willing sister. But two women were not sufficient for his gargantuan appetites. No matter how frequent, or by what multiple the participants and combinations, nothing dimmed his lust for the next experience. As he observed, depravity, what we might call pornography, quickly palls and must be continuously renewed, changed and updated. An erotic book is seldom re-read. Readers require fresh stimulations.

The Marquis famously procured the services of the well-known beauty Rose Keller, then kept her in captivity and sexually abused her for three days. On escaping, she filed a report with the authorities, and only the intervention of de Sade's mother-in-law, a confidante of the Louis XV, prevented him, on this occasion, from being imprisoned.

The scandal did not inhibit de Sade. On the contrary, his infamy in court appears to have been a provocation. He was charged in 1772 for supplying the aphrodisiac Spanish Fly to some prostitutes in Marseilles. During the investigation, he was further accused of sodomy with his manservant, Latour, and sentenced to death *in absentia*. They fled to Italy, de Sade taking Anne-Prospère with him. They were caught, imprisoned by the Italians, and escaped back to France, where the Marquis hid in the castle in Lacoste.

Immune by this time to de Sade's immorality, jealous, perhaps, of her sister, his wife decided to abandon the pious teachings of her childhood and became a willing participant in the castle's nefarious activities, thus proving her husband's theory that erotica is addictive and, no matter how far you go, there is the temptation to go further. Servant girls were deflowered and flogged before fleeing home to their villages, although some remained loyal and eager accomplices for many years. The father of one girl in 1777 arrived at Lacoste to claim his daughter, and, at point-blank range, attempted to shoot the Marquis. The gun misfired.

De Sade had always been lucky, but luck's natural journey is to run out. Later that year, he was captured on a brief visit to Paris. An aristocrat and war hero, he successfully appealed his death sentence, but was imprisoned in the Château de Vincennes. He promptly absconded, a skill well-honed from his various escapades, but was captured again, his jailors placating his penchant for escape by allowing him a generous supply of paper and ink.

De Sade was moved to the Bastille, where he began his opus *Les 120 Journées de Sodome – 120 Days of Sodom*. The manuscript survived his move in 1789 to Charenton, an insane asylum, where, that same year, the French Revolution resulted in the overthrow of the Monarchy. High ranking members of the new Constituent Assembly formed in 1790 were conversant of de Sade's political writing, saw him as a fellow traveler and he was immediately released.

The Marquis gathered his manuscripts, each written on scraps of paper in dark prison cells. They were edited and he saw several of his books published during the first years of the 1790s. His wife had divorced him and the castle at Lacoste was uninhabitable after being sacked by the mob. He took to living with the actress Marie-Constance Quesnet, with whom he would remain for the rest of his life, and returned to his second great passion, politics. In spite of his aristocratic background, he joined the radicals and was elected to the National Convention representing the far left. He wrote political pamphlets and advocated fairer voting systems for the poor and landless, revolutionary ideas for revolutionary times.

He was against the Reign of Terror that saw the execution of King Louis XVI in 1793. He criticized Robespierre, its principal architect, and was again sent to prison, where he remained until the execution of Robespierre a year later. The death of Robespierre brought the Terror to an end and confirmed for de Sade his hatred of state tyranny, the death sentence, and politics in general.

By 1796, all de Sade had to his name was his title. He was forced to sell the ruined castle and looked to his writing to earn a crust. Napoleon came to power in 1801. The General – a frustrated author – ordered the arrest of the 'anonymous' creator of *Justine* and *Juliette*. The finger was pointed at de Sade, as Napoleon knew it would, and the old libertine was sent this time to the old fortress of Bicetre to serve his sentence among cutthroats and assassins.

He had the good fortune to be declared insane by his family and was returned to the insane asylum at Charenton, where he staged several of his plays with inmates acting the parts and Parisian high society making up the audience. De Sade's last great coup, as he saw it, was the seduction of Madeleine Leclerc, the thirteen-year-old daughter of an employee at Charenton, with whom he maintained sexual relations until his death four years later in 1814.

Between the lines of the Marquis de Sade's novels is an analysis of how power and economics relate. The strong overpowering and abusing the weak is a metaphor for the politics of his time, as he noted, 'for all times'. He championed erotica as a literary form and can be seen as the definitive symbol of the artist's struggle against censorship which, it has to be said, he clearly won.

His work is still in print, as popular today as it ever. They are biographies in just about every language and several bio-pics. The best known is the *Quills* (2000), starring Geoffrey Rush, Kate Winslet and Joaquin Phoenix, directed by Philip Kaufman and written by Doug Wright. There are numerous movies based on his work. I would recommend tracking down the splendid 1969 film version of his novel *Justine*, written by Harry Alan Towers, directed by Jesus Franco with Romina Power, Maria Rohm and Klaus Kinski as the Marquis de Sade: 'A woman named Justine is (willingly) used and abused by all manner of perverts, freaks and sexual deviants,' according to IMDB, the Internet Movie Data Base.

PART 3

The Work

of the Marquis de Sade

What follows are two extracts from de Sade's work, the first from *Justine*, the second from *120 Days of Sodom*. The language may be old-fashioned, but the writer's delight in debauchery is abundantly clear.

Justine is considered the Marquis de Sade's greatest novel. The book was a fuller version of an earlier draft, the sadistic and erotic content heightened to reflect de Sade's growing knowledge of the form and as a further challenge to the censors and government.

The version we know today was first published in 1791 and is set shortly before the French revolution. It tells the story of a girl aged twelve who, on a journey across France, is abused, raped and debauched by the men she meets – aristocrats, a judge, the monks at a monastery who make her a sex slave, and all the rogues and perverts who stumble upon her along the way. Originally titled *The Misfortunes of Virtue (Les infortunes de la vertu)*, in *Justine,* the central character has a sister, *Juliette,* whose story is recounted in a later book, the two creating a work of some 4,000 pages and covering every erotic prospect writers in the genre have drawn on ever since.

To avoid her name being sullied, the artifice common to the period, Justine goes under the name 'Therese'. De Sade uses the device of telling the story as a confession made by

Therese to Madame de Lorsagne, a woman she meets in an inn.

- NOTE: in contemporary erotica, the participants are not twelve, they are all over eighteen, there is no spilling of blood and the activities are consensual.

The extract is set in a monastery serving as a sort of finishing school for girls. Therese is recounting to Madame de Lorsagne an orgy involving the monk Antonin and four young girls. What follows is Therese's seduction by Severino, 'the most libertine man of our times', a night with the Clement, who strips her naked, instructs her to 'pass wind' in his mouth, beats her with a birch cane…and so on.

There is a slow build to the erotic content for which the writer is famous, so stay with it:

Extract from Justine

'When one is going to be dismissed, one is notified the same morning, never earlier: as usual, the Officer of the Day makes his appearance at nine o'clock and says, let us suppose, 'Omphale, the monastery is sending you into retirement; I will come to take you this evening.' Then he continues about his business.

But you do not present yourself for his inspection; he examines the others, then he leaves; the person about to be released embraces her comrades, she makes a thousand promises to strive in their behalf, to bring charges, to tell abroad what transpires in the monastery: the hour strikes, the monk appears, the girl is led away, and not a word is heard of her. Supper takes place in the usual fashion; we have simply been able to remark that upon these days the monks rarely reach pleasure's ultimate episodes, one might say they proceed gingerly and with unwonted care. However, they drink a great deal more, sometimes even to inebriation; they send us to our chamber at a much earlier hour, they take no one to bed with them, even the Girls of the Watch are relegated to the seraglios.'

'Very well,' I say to my companion, 'if no one has helped you it is because you have had to deal with frail, intimidated creatures, or women with children who dared not attempt anything for you. That they will kill us is not my fear; at least, I don't believe they do: that reasoning beings could carry crime to that point... it is unthinkable... I know that full well... After what I have seen and undergone I perhaps ought not defend mankind as I do, but, my dear, it is simply inconceivable that they can execute horrors the very idea of which defies the imagination. Oh dear companion!' I pursued with great emotion, 'would you like to exchange that promise which for my part I swear I will fulfill!... Do you wish it ?'

'Yes.'

'Ah, I swear to you in the name of all I hold most holy, in the name of the God Who makes me to breathe and Whom only I adore... I vow to you I will either die in the undertaking or destroy these infamies... will you promise me the same?'

'Do not doubt it,' Omphale replied, 'but be certain of these promises' futility; others more embittered than you, stauncher, no less resolute and not so scrupulous, in a word, friends who would have shed their last drop of blood for us, have not kept identical vows; and so, dear Therese, and so allow my cruel experience to consider ours equally vain and to count upon them no more.'

'And the monks,' I said, 'do they also vary, do new ones often come here?'

'No,' answered Omphale, 'Antonin has been here ten years, Clement eighteen, Jerome thirty, Severino twenty-five. The superior was born in Italy, he is closely allied to the Pope with whom he is in intimate contact; only since his arrival have the so-called miracles of the Virgin assured the monastery's reputation and prevented scandalmongers from observing too closely what takes place here; but when he came the house was already furnished as presently you see it to be; it has subsisted in the same style and upon this footing for above a century, and all the superiors who have governed it have perpetuated a system which so amicably smiles upon their pleasures.

Severino, the most libertine man of our times, has only installed himself here in order to lead a life consonant with his tastes. He intends to maintain this abbey's secret privileges as long as he possibly can. We belong to the diocese of Auxerre, but whether or not the bishop is informed, we never see him, never does he set foot in the monastery: generally speaking, very few outsiders come here except toward the time of the festival which is that of Notre Dame d'Aout; according to the monks, ten persons do not arrive at this house over the period of a twelvemonth; however, it is very likely that when strangers do present themselves, the superior takes care to receive them with hospitality; by appearances of religion and austerity he imposes upon them, they go away content, the monastery is eulogized, and thus these villains' impunity is established upon the people's good faith and the credulity of the devout.'

Omphale had scarcely concluded her instruction when nine o'clock tolled; the superintendent called us to come quickly, and the Officer of the Day did indeed enter. 'Twas Antonin; according to custom, we drew ourselves up in a line. He cast a rapid glance upon the group, counted us, and sat down; then, one by one, we went forward and lifted our skirts, on the one side as high as the navel, on the other up to the middle of the back. Antonin greeted the homage with the unconcern of satiety; then, clapping an eye upon me, he asked how I liked this newest of my adventures. Getting no response but tears,

'She'll manage,' he said with a laugh; 'in all of France there's not a single house where girls are finished as nicely as they are in this.'

From the superintendent's hands he took the list of girls who had misbehaved, then, addressing himself to me again, he caused me to shudder; each gesture, each movement which seemed to oblige me to submit myself to these libertines was for me as a sentence of death.

Antonin commanded me to sit on the edge of a bed and when I was in this posture he bade the superintendent uncover my breast and raise my skirt to above my waist; he himself spread my legs as far apart as possible, he seats himself before this prospect, one of my companions comes and takes up the same pose on top of me in such a way that it is the altar of generation instead of my visage which is offered to Antonin; with these charms raised to the level of his mouth he readies himself for pleasure.

A third girl, kneeling before him, begins to excite him with her hands, and a fourth, completely naked, with her fingers indicates where he must strike my body. Gradually, this girl begins to arouse me and what she does to me Antonin does as well, with both his hands, to two other girls on his left and right. One cannot imagine the language, the obscene speeches by which that debauchee stimulates himself; at last he is in the state he desires, he is led to me, but everyone follows him, moves with him, endeavors to inflame him yet further while he takes his pleasure; his naked hind parts are exposed, Omphale takes possession of them and neglects nothing in order to irritate him: rubbings, kisses, pollutions, she employs them all; completely afire, Antonin leaps toward me....

'I wish to stuff her this time,' he says, beside himself.... These moral deviations determine the physical. Antonin, who has the habit of uttering terrible cries during the final instants of drunkenness, emits dreadful ones; everyone surrounds, everyone serves him, everyone labors to enrich his ecstasy, and the libertine attains it in the midst of the most bizarre episodes of luxury and depravation.

These groupings were frequent; for when a monk indulged in whatever form of pleasure, all the girls regularly surrounded him in order to fire all his parts' sensations, that voluptuousness might, if one may be forgiven the expression, more surely penetrate into him through every pore.

Antonin left, breakfast was brought in; my companions forced me to eat, I did so to please them. We had not quite finished when the superior entered: seeing us still at table, he dispensed us from ceremonies which were to have been identical with those we had just executed for Antonin. 'We must give a thought to dressing her,' said he, looking at me; and then he opened a wardrobe and threw upon my bed several garments of the color appropriate to my class, and several bundles of linen as well.

'Try that on,' he said, 'and give me what belongs to you.'

I donned the new clothes and surrendered my old; but, in anticipation of having to give them up, I had, during the night, prudently removed my money from my pockets and had concealed it in my hair. With each article of clothing I took off, Severino's ardent stare fell upon the feature newly exposed, and his hands wandered to it at once.

At length, when I was half-naked, the monk seized me, put me in the position favorable to his pleasure, that is to say, in the one exactly opposite to the attitude Antonin had made me assume; I wish to ask him to spare me, but spying the fury already kindled in his eyes, I decide the obedient is the safer way; I take my place, the others form a ring around me, Severino is able to see nothing but a multitude of those obscene altars in which he delights; his hands converge upon mine, his mouth fastens upon it, his eyes devour it... he is at the summit of pleasure.

With your approval, Madame, said the beautiful Therese, I shall limit myself to a foreshortened account of the first month I spent in that monastery, that is, I will confine myself to the period's principal anecdotes; the rest would be pure repetition; the monotony of that sojourn would make my recital tedious; immediately afterward, I should, it seems to me, move on to the events which finally produced my emergence from this ghastly sewer.

I did not attend supper that first day; I had simply been selected to pass the night with Dom Clement. In accordance with custom, I was outside his cell some few minutes before he was expected to return to it; the jailer opened the door, then locked it when I had gone in.

Clement arrives as warm with wine as lust, he is followed by the twenty-six year-old girl who, at the time was officiating as his watch; previously informed of what I am to do, I fall to my knees as soon as I hear him coming; he nears me, considers me in my humbled posture, then commands me to rise and kiss him upon the mouth; he savors the kiss for several moments and imparts to it all the expression... all the amplitude one could possibly conceive.

Meanwhile, Armande, as his thrall was named, undresses me by stages; when the lower part of the loins, with which she had begun, is exposed, she bids me turn around and display to her uncle the area his tastes cherish. Clement examines it, feels it, then, reposing himself in an armchair, orders me to bring it close so that he can kiss it; Armande is upon her knees, rousing him with her mouth, Clement places his at the sanctuary of the temple I present to him and his tongue strays into the path situate at its center; his hands fasten upon the corresponding altar in Armande but, as the clothing the girl is still wearing impedes him, he commands her to be rid of it, this is soon done, and the docile creature returns to her uncle to take up a position in which, while exciting him with only the hand, she finds herself better within reach of Clement's.

The impure monk uninterruptedly occupied with me in like fashion, then tells me to give the largest possible vent to whatever winds may be hovering in my bowels, and these I am to direct into his mouth; this eccentricity struck me as revolting, but I was at the time far from perfect acquaintance with all the irregularities of debauch: I obey and straightway feel the effect of this intemperance.

More excited, the monk becomes more impassioned: he suddenly applies bites to six different places upon the fleshy globes I have put at his disposal; I emit a cry and start forward involuntarily, whereat he stands, advances toward me, rage blazing in his eyes, and demands whether I know what I am risking by unsettling him.... I make a thousand apologies, he grasps the corset still about my torso, rips it away, and my blouse too, in less time than it takes to tell....

Ferociously he seizes my breasts, spouting invectives as he squeezes, wrings, crushes them; Armande undresses him, and there we are, all three of us, naked. Upon Armande his attention comes to bear for a moment: he deals her savage blows with his fists; kisses her mouth; nibbles her tongue and lips, she screams; pain now and again sends the girl into uncontrollable gales of weeping; he has her stand upon a chair and extracts from her just what he desired from me.

Armande satisfies him, with one hand I excite him, and, during this luxury, I whip him gently with the other, he also bites Armande, but she holds herself somehow in check, not daring to stir a hair. The monster's tooth-marks are soon printed upon the lovely girl's flesh; they are to be seen in a number of places; brusquely wheeling upon me:

'Therese,' he says, 'you are going to suffer cruelly' He had no need to tell me so, for his eyes declared it but too emphatically. 'You are going to be lashed everywhere,' he continues, 'everywhere, without exception,' and as he spoke he again laid hands upon my breasts and mauled them brutally, he bruised their extremities with his fingertips and occasioned me very sharp pain; I dared not say a word for fear of irritating him yet more, but sweat bathed my forehead and, willy-nilly, my eyes filled with tears; he turns me about, makes me kneel on the edge of a chair upon whose back I must keep my hands without removing them for a single instant; he promises to inflict the gravest penalties upon me if I lift them; seeing me ready and well within range, he orders Armande to fetch him some birch rods, she presents him with a handful, slender and long.

Clement snatches them, and recommending that I not stir, he opens with a score of stripes upon my shoulders and the small of my back; he leaves me for an instant, returns to Armande, brings her back, she too is made to kneel upon a chair six feet from where I am; he declares he is going to flog us simultaneously and the first of the two to release her grip, utter a cry, or shed a tear will be exposed on the spot to whatever torture he is pleased to inflict: he bestows the same number of strokes upon Armande he has just given me, and positively upon the identical places, he returns to me, kisses everything he has just left off molesting, and raising his sticks, says to me, 'Steady, little slut, you are going to be used like the last of the damned.'

Whereupon I receive fifty strokes, all of them directed between the region bordered by the shoulders and the small of the back. He dashes to my comrade and treats her likewise: we pronounce not a word; nothing may be heard but a few stifled groans, we have enough strength to hold back our tears.

There was no indication as to what degree the monk's passions were inflamed; he periodically excited himself briskly, but nothing rose. Returning now to me, he spent a moment eyeing those two fatty globes then still intact but about to undergo torture in their turn; he handled them, he could not prevent himself from prying them apart, tickling them, kissing them another thousand times.

'Well,' said he, 'be courageous...' and a hail of blows descended upon these masses, lacerating them to the thighs. Extremely animated by the starts, the leaps, the grinding of teeth, the contortions the pain drew from me, examining them, battening upon them rapturously, he comes and expresses, upon my mouth which he kisses with fervor, the sensations agitating him....

'This girl entertains me,' he cries, 'I have never flogged another with as much pleasure,' and he goes back to his niece whom he treats with the same barbarity; there remained the space between the upper thigh and the calves and this he struck with identical vehemence: first the one of us, then the other.

'Ha!' he said, now approaching me, 'let's change hands and visit this place here'. Now wielding a cat-o'-nine-tails he gives me twenty cuts from the middle of my belly to the bottom of my thighs; then wrenching them apart, he slashed at the interior of the lair my position bares to his whip. 'There it is,' says he, 'the bird I am going to pluck': several thongs having, through the precautions he had taken, penetrated very deep, I could not suppress my screams.

'Well, well!' said the villain, 'I must have found the sensitive area at last; steady there, calm yourself, we'll visit it a little more thoroughly'.

However, his niece is put in the same posture and treated in the same manner; once again he reaches the most delicate region of a woman's body; but whether through habit, or courage, or dread of incurring treatment yet worse, she has enough strength to master herself, and about her nothing is visible beyond a few shivers and spasmodic twitching. However, there was by now a slight change in the libertine's physical aspect, and although things were still lacking in substance, thanks to stroking and shaking a gradual improvement was being registered.

'On your knees,' the monk said to me, 'I am going to whip your titties.'

'My titties, oh my Father!'

'Yes, those two lubricious masses which never excite me but I wish to use them thus,' and upon saying this, he squeezed them, he compressed them violently.

'Oh Father! They are so delicate! You will kill me!'

'No matter, my dear, provided I am satisfied,' and he applied five or six blows which, happily, I parried with my hands. Upon observing that, he binds them behind my back; nothing remains with which to implore his mercy but my countenance and my tears, for he has harshly ordered me to be silent. I strive to melt him... but in vain, he strikes out savagely at my now unprotected bosom; terrible bruises are immediately writ out in black and blue; blood appears as his battering continues, my suffering wrings tears from me, they fall upon the vestiges left by the monster's rage, and render them, says he, yet a thousand times more interesting... he kisses those marks, he devours them and now and again returns to my mouth, to my eyes whose tears he licks up with lewd delight.

Armande takes her place, her hands are tied, she presents breasts of alabaster and the most beautiful roundness; Clement pretends to kiss them, but to bite them is what he wishes.... And then he lays on and that lovely flesh, so white, so plump, is soon nothing more in its butcher's eyes but lacerations and bleeding stripes.

'Wait one moment,' says the berserk monk, 'I want to flog simultaneously the most beautiful of behinds and the softest of breasts.'

He leaves me on my knees and, bringing Armande toward me, makes her stand facing me with her legs spread, in such a way that my mouth touches her womb and my breasts are exposed between her thighs and below her behind; by this means the monk has what he wants before him: Armande's buttocks and my titties in close proximity: furiously he beats them both, but my companion, in order to spare me blows which are becoming far more dangerous for me than for her, has the goodness to lower herself and thus shield me by receiving upon her own person the lashes that would inevitably have wounded me.

Clement detects the trick and separates us: 'She'll gain nothing by that,' he fumes, 'and if today I have the graciousness to spare that part of her, 'twill only be so as to molest some other at least as delicate.'

As I rose I saw that all those infamies had not been in vain: the debauchee was in the most brilliant state; and it made him only the more furious; he changes weapons He opens a cabinet where several martinets are to be found and draws out one armed with iron tips. I fall to trembling. 'There, Therese,' says he showing me the martinet, 'you'll see how delicious it is to be whipped with this... you'll feel it, you'll feel it, my rascal, but for the instant I prefer to use this other one...'

It was composed of small knotted cords, twelve in all; at the end of each was a knot somewhat larger than the others, about the size of a plum pit. 'Come there! Up! The cavalcade!... the cavalcade!' says he to his niece; she, knowing what is meant, quickly gets down on all fours, her rump raised as high as possible, and tells me to imitate her; I do.

Clement leaps upon my back, riding facing my rear; Armande, her own presented to him, finds herself directly ahead of Clement: the villain then discovering us both well within reach, furiously cuts at the charms we offer him; but, as this position obliges us to open as wide as possible that delicate part of ourselves which distinguishes our sex from men's, the barbarian aims stinging blows in this direction: the whip's long and supple strands, penetrating into the interior with much more facility than could withes or ferules, leave deep traces of his rage; now he strikes one, now his blows fly at the other; as skilled a horseman as he is an intrepid flagellator, he several times changes his mount; we are exhausted, and the pangs of pain are of such violence that it is almost impossible to bear them any longer.

'Stand up,' he tells us, catching up the martinet again, 'yes, get up and stand in fear of me' His eyes glitter, foam flecks his lips He like persons distracted, we run about the room, here, there, he follows after us, indiscriminately striking Armande, myself; the villain brings us to blood; at last he traps us both between the bed and the wall: the blows are redoubled: the unhappy Armande receives one upon the breast which staggers her, this last horror determines his ecstasy, and while my back is flailed by its cruel effects, my loins are flooded by the proofs of a delirium whose results are so dangerous.

Extract from 120 Days of Sodom

This scene from 120 Days of Sodom is narrated by Françon, a young orphan girl living under the protection of the church.

One day as I was entering church, Father Louis sidled up to me and asked me to come to his room. Scarcely were we inside when he bolted the door and, having poured some elixir into a goblet, bade me swallow it. This predatory step taken, the Reverend fell to kissing me and fondling my posterior. Then, raising my skirt to my bodice, he asked me if I did not desire to pee. Singularly driven to this need by the drink he had given me, I assured him the urge to do so was powerful, but I did not want to satisfy this need in front of him.

'Oh, my goodness do,' he cried, 'by God, yes; pee in my presence and, what's more, you can pee upon my prick. Here it is,' he added, plucking it from his breeches, 'here is the tool you are going to moisten. Piss on it now.'

He lifted me up and set me between two chairs, then invited me to squat. Holding me in this position, he placed a container beneath me and held his prick between the container and my cunt.

'Off you go, little one, piss,' he urged, 'flood my prick with your enchanting liquid whose hot descent exerts such a sway over my senses, Piss, my heart, and inundate my come.'

The ecclesiastic now began to beat at his prick with insane vigor. It was easy to see that this curious pissing operation was that which his senses most cherished. The sweetest, gentlest ecstasy crowned his face as the liquid with which he had swollen my stomach flowed most abundantly out of me and we simultaneously filled the same pot, he with sperm, I with piss.

The exercise concluded, Father Louis delivered roughly the same speech to me which I had heard from Father Laurent: he wished to make me a procuress. Motivated by his generous payment, I boldly guided every young girl I knew to him. He had every one of them do the same thing, and, since he experienced no compunctions about seeing any one of them a second time, I found myself with a tidy little sum of money.

Thus we come to see that, once corrupted, Françon becomes a corrupter.

PART 4

Contemporary Erotica

What follows are selections from *The Girl Quintet,* my five novels, each written with a flavor of de Sade, the contemporary feel of EL James and young female protagonists, not unlike Anastasia Steele, finding their way into the mystery of their own sexuality.

Quite aside from being proud of my books, the extracts are a learning tool for new writers. I would suggest reading them twice, once quickly, to get the feel, then slowly, deconstructing the elements to see how character traits are concealed in the subtext and sex evolves, not gratuitously, but through plot.

In the United States, the United Kingdom and Australia, the copyright of written work lasts until 70 years after the writer's death (50 years in Canada). EL James, indeed all living writers, guard their publications and want readers to buy their work, not download it or reproduce it without consent. The Marquis de Sade's writing can be found for free on the web. Ironically, he died in poverty.

The first excerpt is a chapter from the novel *Being A Girl,* published in 2007 by Nexus and available as a paperback and digital download. Do visit **www.chloethurlow.com** for details of all my books.

The following comes from the chapter entitled *Men in Kilts,* innocence meets a dominant aristocrat and the reader should be left wondering whether being corrupted is more pleasure than pain.

Back-cover blurb:

A journey of discovery and awakening to the delights of discipline.

When Milly is late for a vital interview on a sweltering day, casting agent Jean-Luc Cartier pours her some water and holds the glass to her lips. When the water soaks her blouse he instructs her to take it off. Milly is embarrassed but curious. As Milly strips off her clothes, not only her shapely body, but also her deepest nature, is slowly uncovered.

Jean-Luc puts her over his knee. He spanks her bottom and her virgin orgasm awakens her to the mysteries of discipline. Milly embark upon an erotic journey from convent school to a black magic coven in the heart of Cambridge academia, to the secret world of fetishism and bondage on the dark side of the movie camera.

Men in Kilts

Binky and I had always had a strange, not to say strained relationship. Of course we love each other. That's why we hate each other. It's what happens when sisters are born less than a year apart. She was already as tall as me, which was totally unfair, and her killer legs in the shortest skirts in London had roofers falling from scaffolds and myopic pedestrians walking into lamp posts. We were born to be rivals, and in our race into the adult world, she had taken the lead. At least, that's what she wanted everyone to think.

Added to her porcelain skin and classic good looks, my sister had the self-confidence of those who *always* get their own way. She was *a real cutie*. That's what her driving instructor said when he called her and spoke to me by accident. I thought she was an awful driver but she had managed to pass her test first time after only five lessons and had acquired a pink VW beetle with 'African violet trim' from a friend of the driving examiner. The plot thickens.

Anyway, she hunted me down in Notting Hill one Saturday when I was supposed to be looking for a summer job and almost crashed into an elderly gent in an electric wheelchair. Binky zoomed into a vacant parking spot, gestured hopelessly towards the poor old gentleman and rushed me into the *King's Head* for a buck's fizz, her latest discovery.

She strolled up to the bar in her pink Doc Marten's and behaved as if she wasn't enjoying the heads turning to watch the sway of her perfectly round bottom. If anyone was a little tart it was my sister Binky.

She turned her shoulder to one side as she cast her green eyes on the barman.

'Two bucks fizz, please,' she said in her plummy accent.

'Here, you old enough, darling?' I heard the barman say.

'What a cheek,' she replied, and the barman grinned as he added orange juice to the champagne flutes.

Binky since the start of the summer hols had gone retro with her gelled hair, a slashed tee-shirt and a little skirt that would have made our poor matron turn in her grave, if she were dead of course.

'You're becoming such a slut, Binky,' I hissed as she set the glasses on a vacant table.

'You can talk,' she said, and I blushed.

I had told Binky *everything* that had happened that day in Monsieur Cartier's office and I wasn't sure whether she believed me or not. When I looked back, I didn't quite believe it myself, although a rosy glow had stained my bottom for ages and when I closed my eyes and pictured myself wriggling naked on his lap my insides went all watery.

While I was squirming on the hard wooden seat, Binky was pressing a finger to her lips and I could almost visualize all the little cogs whirring around in her mind. She leaned forward and looked deadly serious.

'Have you found a job yet?' she asked.

'No,' I answered.

Her eyes grew big. 'We're going to go away for a holiday,' she said, 'and if you don't come, Milly, I'll never speak to you again.'

I took another sip of champagne and the bubbles made me giggle as they went up my nose.

'I don't want to speak to you anyway,' I said, and she drummed her nails on the tabletop until I continued. 'All right,' I added, 'where?'

'As far away as possible,' she said breathlessly. 'Let's go to Scotland.'

'Scotland?'

'Yes, Scotland. We've never been there,' she said. 'You like doing things you've never done before, don't you?'

She turned sideways in her seat and slapped the side of her bottom.

'Only if it's fun.'

'Well, you never know unless you try.'

'I don't know...'

'Please, Milly, please. I'm dying to try out my car...'

'Have you had it serviced?' I asked. I was the practical one.

'Yes, *matron*, everything's ticketyboo.'

She placed her pink boots up on the bench beside me and her skirt slipped over her thighs.

'Everyone can see your knickers,' I said and she sighed contentedly.

'They're new,' she replied, and sipped her bucks fizz.

We were supposed to be looking for summer jobs, but Daddy had gone back to whatever it was he did for the EU in Brussels; Mummy was having an affair, and in the midst of these passions she didn't mind what we did, as long as we didn't make any noise. Anyway, I deserved a break after the exams and raised my glass in a toast.

'To Scotland.'

We finished our drinks and I felt quite tipsy as I watched Binky skip between the cars back across the road to her pink Volkswagen. I had an interview for a job in a shoe shop and thought I'd let the *fickle finger of fate* decide on my future: if I got the job I would stay in London and, if I didn't, I would go on an adventure with my little sister.

I wandered off to the tube thinking about smelly feet. I was ten minutes late for the interview and was told by the woman who called herself Madame Dubarry that I was obviously "spoiled" from having gone to boarding school and didn't have the right "attitude" to devote myself to the shoe trade.

She was shaking her head and peering unpleasantly at my chest. 'Selling shoes requires a certain discipline,' she said. 'You are clearly cut out for other *better* things.'

'I'm sure I am,' I said sullenly and had a real spring in my step as I marched off to the map shop in Long Acre.

During the coming days, I plotted the route, and Binky acquired a pair of pink flairs to go with her Doc Marten's. We set off the following weekend from Chelsea, up the motorway, and over the sea to Skye, which really was as beautiful as I'd imagined. We had a two-man tent and planned to camp, although I did have my doubts about Binky roughing it with her long nails and creamy white skin, much of which was on display in her Che Guevara tee-shirt.

I had dressed appropriately in walking shoes and a heavy sweater. Binky had made fun of my get-up on the long drive, but it turned out that I had made the right choice. We had left London early to avoid the jams and crossed to Skye just before six. It had been warm and sunny all day, but Scotland, we discovered, had its own way of doing things.

We were driving west between high stone walls, the narrow lanes curvy and deserted. The sky grew darker and when the clouds ripped apart in a flash of lightening, we screamed as great hailstones the size of tennis balls started beating on the windscreen. The car misted up. The wipers were slowing, and when the engine conked out, the wipers froze solid and we couldn't see a thing.

We sat there for an hour. Binky wriggled into her sleeping bag and we watched the hail turning gradually to rain. The storm was passing, but when my sister went to start the car, it was dead. We got out and peered at the engine, the jumble of wires and rubber tubes sitting there all wet and cold, a complete and absolute mystery.

'Typical!' I said.

'What is?'

'African violet trim,' I mocked. 'Where did you get this car from, anyway?'

'You know perfectly well where I got it from.'

'How much did you pay for it?'

'I exchanged it...'

'What for?

'I'm not telling you.'

She didn't need to tell me. Her cheeks were as red as her tee-shirt. Binky really had grown up, and you didn't have to be a nuclear scientist to know why.

'I knew this would happen,' I said.

'How did you?' she demanded.

'Because something like this always happens.'

'I thought you wanted to have some fun.'

'This wasn't what I had in mind when we left.'

'I did,' she said, and looked back at me with a scornful expression. 'You're such a virgin, Milly.'

I took a deep breath. She had made her point. It was only a breakdown, after all. We had set out in search of adventure, and this was where it all began.

Binky slammed the lid shut and tried the car once more. Nothing. She slipped her arms into her Afghan coat and pulled her big woolly hat over her eyes.

'Are you ready?'

'For anything,' I said, and she smiled.

We glanced back along the lane, but couldn't remember having passed any houses for ages and it was too boring to retrace our steps. I zipped myself into my sensible parka and we set out in the direction we'd been going. We had our mobile phones but weren't sure who to call.

Further along the lane, we saw a building in the middle of a field. It had started to rain again and we were afraid the storm was returning. 'Come on,' Binky said, and she was already climbing the wall. I did have a faint hope that it was a farmhouse where an old lady with her hair rolled into a bun would be busy making scones, but it turned out to be a stone barn, the doors securely bolted. The sky had darkened and the rain was getting heavier. We walked around the outside of the building, but the windows were small and too high to reach.

'What are we going to do?' I said, as Binky vanished around the corner.

She came back carrying an enormous rock and loomed over the new padlock.

'Don't,' I screamed.

But it was too late. She brought it down cleanly on the hasp and as the silver lock sprang open she turned to me with a look of wonder in her green eyes. We were standing close and Binky did something totally unexpected: she leaned forward and pressed her lips playfully to mine. It wasn't a snog, just a peck, but she had never done anything like that before. Her lips were soft but firm and left a sweet taste that lingered on my senses.

'That's disgusting,' I said.

'Liar,' she shot back.

The Fifty Shades of Grey Phenomena

I pulled the door open and we shared the thrill of entering the unknown. The barn was dry with bales of hay stored in steps around the walls. Binky in one swift movement sprinted the length of the barn, vaulted a pile of bales stacked three high and landed perfectly, feet together. Binky was a good gymnast and had never quite seen the point of team games like hockey and Lacrosse where the praise was shared. I clapped my hands and, as Binky caught her breath, we stood there in silence, not quite sure what to do. The slate grey sky was lit by golden streaks of lightning and the sound of the rain running off the roof reminded me that I had not been to the bathroom since the motorway services.

'I'm dying to use the loo,' I said.

'Me too.'

Binky grinned. She was turning the breakdown into an escapade, and that old sense of fun came back to me as we squatted down on our private bales of hay.

I peed for ages.

'Wow, I needed that,' I gasped.

'So I see,' she screamed, and it was totally embarrassing because she was standing there staring at me as I was still peeing. 'Look at the steam. Or is that Scotch mist?'

She spoke with a Scottish accent, and while we erupted in fits of giggles, the shock of a flashlight shining on me before I could pull up my jeans came as such a surprise I tripped and fell back in the hay. Binky laughed as she wriggled into her flares and we turned, blinded by the light.

'What have we here then, some vagrants?'

It was a man's voice, the tone stern but melodic, his rrrs rolling poetically. The torchlight ran over us like eager hands.

'We're lost,' Binky said in her little girl voice. 'Our car broke down...'

'You're trespassing on private property.'

Binky dropped her head to one side. 'Can you help us?' she pleaded.

'Just the two of you, are there?' the man asked, the flashlight probing the corners of the barn. 'No other vagrants hiding in the hay?'

'No, just us.'

He shined the light on me. 'You're the quiet one, are you, the dark horse?'

'No…'

'Well, now, we'd better see what the Laird has to say. He knows how to deal with young girls.'

'We haven't done anything,' I said,

'Aye,' he replied as he led us out and closed the barn doors.

He pocketed the broken lock. We climbed into the muddy Land Rover parked outside, and I thought at least we were going somewhere safe and warm. We sat in the back holding hands. The man was whistling to himself, and drove for ages over dark fields that looked like the sea at night, on and on, and it was a relief when a big manor house came into view in a dip between the hills. There was a warm light behind the ground floor windows and I squeezed Binky's fingers to show her I was enjoying myself.

The man opened the car. He urged us up the steps and we passed through the high arched doors into a wood-paneled hallway. He hung his waterproofs on the stand, and I noticed now that he was wearing a kilt, the pleats swaying hypnotically above sturdy calves as we followed him along the passage below the glassy eyes of numerous stags' heads. He stopped at a closed door and rapped with his knuckles.

'You can wait here,' he said.

He went in and we looked at each other. Binky grinned, and as she raised her thin shoulders, I knew she was busy inventing some excuse for breaking into the barn.

When the man opened the door, we entered a baronial hall dominated by a big log fire roaring between pillars of marble. There were various pieces of dark, heavy furniture:

chests, a sideboard, a black piano. The extended dining table was framed by tall windows, and wood smoke clung in the defiles between the beams on the ceiling. Crossed swords and old blunderbusses decorated the walls among portraits of stern men with red beards and dour women who gazed out with severe unforgiving expressions. Above the fire was a life-sized painting of a beautiful woman with dark hair and dark unfathomable eyes.

Like the men in the portraits, the man in the winged armchair at the fireside was red-bearded, his hands dwarfing the leather bound book he was holding. He showed no interest in us as we stood before him. He finished reading to the end of the page before closing the volume. He stretched out his long legs, his feet crossed at the ankles. He was dressed in the classical Scottish way with a short black jacket, a dark plaid kilt and a ruffled shirt. His laced shoes nestled in the fleece surrounding the hearth and the sporran resting in his lap was the size of a small dog.

'Are you related by any chance to the Laird Hamish of the Black Watch?' He spoke quietly and seemed genuinely puzzled.

We shook our heads, and he raised his voice.

'I didnae hear you. Are you deaf?'

'No.'

'No.'

'I didnae think so. I'm the Laird Hamish of the Black Watch and I didnae believe you had naught to do with me.'

'We were just...'

Binky started speaking, cooing in her little voice, but he cut her off, holding up a huge hand the size of a dinner plate. 'Can you kindly speak when you're spoken to,' he said, and turned to the other man; he was similarly dressed in full Scottish attire. 'Byron, did you get those logs in like I asked you?'

'You know I didnae, Milord.'

'Then what are you waiting for, mon? There's no time like the present.'

Byron nodded. The Laird opened his book and we scurried towards the door.

'And one more thing,' he called, 'will you have Mrs. McTavish find that mobile phone. Damn thing's got a mind of its own.'

We were led through to the back of the house and set to work carrying logs from the pile at the end of the yard into the shed attached to the kitchen. It wasn't at all polite to be treated in this way. It fact, it was very rude indeed and should have warned me what to expect. It did go through my mind that we should make our way back to the road, but it was a blustery night and we were miles from anywhere.

We caught a glimpse of Mrs. McTavish fussing about the big iron range and the smell of the food rising from the pots made my tummy rumble. We'd had a sandwich at lunchtime and I was famished.

'Do you think he's going to invite us to dinner?' I whispered, and Binky was as confident as ever.

'Course he is. He's just making us do a bit of work first,' she replied. She hefted up a big pile of logs. 'Builds up the appetite.'

'We mustn't antagonize him, though,' I said, but she was wandering up the path, and if she heard she didn't answer.

When the job was done, we trooped back to the hall. The fire had been built up and Mrs. McTavish was setting three places at the long table.

'What shall we do with these two young criminals, Mrs. McTavish?'

'What?'

'I said what shall we do with these two?'

'There's nae need to shout,' the woman said angrily.

'If I didnae shout you wouldnae hear. You're as deaf as a post, woman.'

'I know what you said, mon, and you know what I think: girls who are disobedient need discipline.'

'That's what my father taught me, Mrs. McTavish.'

'Aye,' she said darkly, 'and me an' all.'

Her words hung in the air and the Laird nodded, considering the remark. 'Thank you and bless you, Mrs. McTavish,' he then said, and held up a mobile phone that looked about the size a postage stamp between his enormous fingers.

When she left, Byron returned, closing the door. The Laird was warming his backside. Byron was tall, at least six foot, but the Laird must have been several inches taller. He continued to look at us while he spoke to his servant. 'What's wrong with you, mon, don't we have a place to hang coats in this hoose?'

'Aye, that we do.'

Byron approached as we removed our coats. He glanced at Binky's hat, she pulled it off, and he hurried out with everything in his arms.

'I suppose you expect Mrs. McTavish to clean up after you, do you?'

'No.'

'No.'

'Then take off your shoes and put them by the fire.'

I did so, standing on one leg. Binky was wearing her pink boots; she sat on the floor to pull them off, the Laird watching as if she were performing a trick. We put our footwear and damp socks by the fire where we'd been told and stood with our backs straight like naughty schoolgirls.

'Now, yoo, blondie, what's your name?' asked the Laird.

'Roberta,' said Binky formally.

'So, Roberta, what's this?' he asked, producing the broken padlock from his sporran.'

'It was an accident.'

'You destroy my property and call it an accident.' He glanced at Byron, back now at his position by the door. 'You hear what they're telling me. It's my fault for having a locked barn.'

'That's the English, Milord.'

The big man stood back as if he'd been struck. 'So, you're from England, now are you?' He was concentrating on Binky, terrorizing her.

'From London,' she said in a whisper.

'Look, we haven't done anything,' I said firmly, and he cut me off.

'Yoo, lassie, you speak when you're spoken to.'

A shiver ran through me as he focused once more on my sister. 'I went there once and I didnae like it. Everyone tearing aboot.' He stared down at her flares. 'You call those bell-bottoms, I suppose.'

She nodded.

'Can you see what they're doing to my polished floor?'

She looked down. 'Dripping a bit,' she answered.

'Shall I call Mrs. McTavish to come and clean up after you?'

She shook her head and swallowed. 'No, of course not...'

'Then take them off, lassie, and hang them here where they can dry.'

She stood there for a long time, eyes down, afraid to look at the Laird with his sharp eyes on her.

'It must be that terrible traffic doon there in London that's made you deaf,' he roared, and Binky glanced at me, trembling as her hands went instinctively to the low slung waist of her flares. She released the belt, unpopped the buttons, and wriggled her bottom as she pulled them down, sliding one at a time out of the legs and hanging the flares by the fire.

The Laird spent like an hour studying her long white legs and then pointed to a straight-backed dining chair. 'Sit,' he said, and she did so.

He turned his concentration to me. 'I suppose it was your idea to climb my walls and trespass on my property. Did you break the lock on my barn?'

'No. Yes. I mean...'

'You're not even sure. You gained entrance to my wee barn and what do you do, you soil the hay with your piddle.' I hung my head. 'Now, lassie, what would you do aboot this criminal behavior on our wee island if you were in my shoes?'

I looked down at his shoes. They were huge; he had the biggest feet I had ever seen. His kilt was the same color as the flames climbing up the chimney, fiery red with maroon stripes running across vertical lines the same shade of African violet as the trim on the car. I could smell the heady scent of pine and wood smoke. Steam was rising from Binky's flares. I looked up with a hopeless shrug.

'I don't know,' I finally managed.

'You've committed a crime.'

'I didn't mean to.'

'Ignorance is no excuse in the eyes of the law, lassie,' he said. 'You may be able to get away with this behavior in London. Not here.'

He turned to warm his big hands and I felt a tingle of fear run up my spine, fear and déjà vu. The Laird turned back and faced me again, feet apart, hands behind his back, the pose of an old-fashioned policeman.

'Take your blouse off, lassie.'

The words entered the room as if from a distance. Of course Mister Cartier that day in his office had started out saying the same thing. That's where it had started; that's where it always starts, I imagined. But it was different this time.

There was no escape. We were in the Laird's clutches. He could do whatever he wanted. My throat felt constricted and my heart was hammering inside my chest.

'Please,' I said eventually. 'I'll pay for the lock.'

'You'll pay?'

'Yes, of course. Anything.'

'You hear that, Byron: anything, she said. Do you believe her?'

'I wouldnae like to say, Milord.'

'I will. Honest.'

Again we were silent. His eyes drilled into me. 'Take off your blouse,' he said. His voice now was melodious, almost playful.

'I didn't mean that...'

He laughed. 'Ah, you see, Byron, you were right. You've never been right before, but this time you're right. You should write it doon in your diary.' The Laird recovered his mobile phone from somewhere inside his kilt. 'What's the number of Sergeant Doyle?'

'It's in the phone, I told you. You just press the letter P.'

'Why's it P and not D, for heaven's sake, mon?'

Byron didn't answer.

The Laird stared down at the machine, his huge digit hovering over the keyboard. I wasn't sure how things had got to this position, and the last thing I wanted was the police to get involved over some silly offence, ruining my chance of going to Cambridge before I'd even been offered a place. He pressed the appropriate key and lifted the phone to his ear.

'Please,' I said.

He stared back at me, his brow crinkled, a smile emerging from his beard.

'Ah, there you are, mon. It's Hamish the Black Watch...'

He listened.

'Aye, and a good evening to you, Sergeant. I wanted to report there's a couple of trespassers on my property, a couple of lassies...'

He watched as my fingers hurried like scuttling insects for the buttons on my blouse, unhooking the first.

There was another pause.

'We can probably handle it in the normal way.'

I undid another button while he nodded into the phone. Then a third.

'Aye, mon, and a very pleasant night for it,' he said, and closed the machine.

The Laird sat back in his winged armchair, watching me. I had undone all the buttons on my blouse and stood with my hands clasping the front together. I glanced at Binky. She was staring at the floor. It was typical that she had broken the lock and I was standing there half undressed. The fine hair on her legs was golden in the firelight. I suppose in a way it was because she had taken off her flares that I had agreed to the humiliation of removing my blouse. Not that I had taken it off yet. I looked automatically back at the Laird and it was like he could read my mind.

'Aye, lassie,' he said.

He spoke softly, kindly, his voice not booming but soothing, a chant. The room was lit by an orange glow. The sky outside was slowly darkening, the long July day turning to night. I peeled the blouse from my shoulders, down my arms and held it in front of me.

'Over here,' he said, pointing at the mesh grille around the fireside.

I hung the blouse beside Binky's flares.

'What's your name, girl?'

'Milly Belladolce.'

'So, you have the hot blood of a Latin in your veins, do you,' he said, and thought about that for a moment. 'Why did you do it, Milly? What possessed you?

'What?'

'If you were caught short you could have gone outside. But oh no, you have to piddle on my property.'

'I'm sorry,' I murmured.

I knew it didn't matter what I said. The Laird of the Black Watch had power over us and was enjoying it.

'So you're sorry, are you?

'Yes, really.'

'And you'll do anything?'

I didn't answer and he glanced again at Byron.

'I did hear right, or am I going deaf like Mrs. McTavish?'

Byron sniffed and changed positions. 'I'll do anything. That's what I heard.'

'It's just an itzy wee thing, Milly. Indulge an old hill farmer who doesnae understand your London ways.'

He didn't say what the itzy wee thing was. He didn't need to. He was just a dirty old man. He wanted me to take off my bra, but if that wasn't bad enough, what I couldn't understand was that the fear had made my breasts swell and my nipples had hardened. I could feel them tingling, pushing against the soft fabric. My breasts were betraying me. My breasts were traitors.

A log broke and sparks chased up the chimney. It gave us something to watch, but once the fire settled it was like the interval in a play was over and the curtain had risen again. My mouth was dry, and mechanically my skinny arms doubled behind my back, my damp nervous fingers slipped the hook from the hasp, and the straps of my bra fell from my shoulders.

No one spoke, but the room appeared to sigh. I went of my own accord to the fireside and dropped the little white fold of fabric on top of my blouse. When I went back to where I had been standing, my first instinct was to slump forward in shame, but I didn't. I straightened my shoulders and even bowed my back a little, stretching my sides. My breasts stood out proud from my chest, high and rounded, the rosy buds so painful I wanted to reach for them, soothe the ache, and it was only willpower that kept my hands modestly behind my back.

The mood had changed. The fire seemed warmer. The Laird stood. Byron moved forward, and the two men studied my breasts as if they had never seen breasts before. I really wasn't sure why men had this obsession.

'Now, lassie, doesn't that feel better?' the Laird asked. His tone was soft, rhythmic, the voice of someone used to being obeyed.

I don't know why I nodded my head but I did, and he appeared so pleased I thought I'd scored a valuable point. I hated being exposed like this, my breasts being scrutinized, but the absurdity of the situation, even the faint awe in the faces of the two men, calmed my nerves and made me feel vaguely superior. Binky was sitting on the edge of the chair, staring at me intensely. The Laird observed her gaze, and when he turned to her it was obvious what was going to happen next.

'Now, lassie,' he said. 'What are you hiding down that wee shirt of yours? You havenae been swiping my antique snuff boxes while I wasnae looking?'

She shook her head.

'Then let's not delay more than's necessary. Off it comes girl. On your feet.'

Her cheeks were flushed. Her flat tummy was going in and out as she stood, her breasts throbbing. It was odd but, like the Laird, like Byron, I was now waiting in the same salacious way to see her strip down to her underwear. She shrugged, trying to look blasé, and as I'd always been good at reading my sister, I had the impression that she was competing with me, that she didn't want to be outdone in any way.

She stretched her arms to pull the tee-shirt over hear head. She shook her blonde hair free, and as she placed the shirt by the fire, the Laird raised his bushy eye-brows, nodding just slightly. There was no escaping his meaning.

Binky lingered for a moment, slipped the bra straps from her shoulders and lowered the strips of material over her elbows. She turned, not really meaning to wiggle, and her breasts quivered seductively as she unhooked the clasp. Her heart, I knew, was pounding, and it made her white breasts tremble all the more.

She dropped the bra on the pile and stood at my side, fragile and defenseless wearing nothing but little knickers, the few wisps of hair escaping from around the elastic all the more endearing. The Laird approached and stood towering over us, legs apart, hands on hips, his eyes flicking between our breasts.

'Now, isn't that better girls?' he said, but he didn't expect an answer. 'What do you think, Byron, have you ever seen finer titties? It must be something in the water they've got doon there in London.'

Byron stood at his master's side, gazing at our breasts in the same studious manner. The room was hot, the fire roaring. I was perspiring. I could smell fear and anticipation on my skin. I had no idea what this big man was going to do to us and I realized at that moment he really could do anything he wanted. No one knew where we were. We were lost on a dark night and my breasts tingled, my nipples pointing at him like two accusing fingers. I looked up into his eyes and he smiled as he scratched the thick red hair on his cheek.

'Look, now, mon, we have a dark one and a light one.' He leaned back and shook his head. 'Same height, too.'

'That's useful,' said Byron, nodding with approval as he glanced up at the beams on the ceiling.

Later I would know what they were talking about. The damp on my back formed a bead of sweat that ran down my spine. The fire roared. My breasts were full and heavy, my breath threading the silence like a needle passing through silk.

I glanced down: my pink nipples had turned dark like ripe plums and hummed as if with a charge of electricity. I was wet and tremulous, the Laird's soft voice like a prayer when he spoke.

'Slip those trousers off like a good girl, now. Just like your wee friend.'

I swallowed hard. I didn't want to, but Binky was standing there in nothing but her knickers and I rationalized that it was only fair. I looked up into the Laird's eyes and got the odd sensation that I was about to sit on a mat at the top of the helter-skelter, and once I pushed off I would slide into oblivion.

'No,' I said, softly, without conviction.

'I don't want to fight you, lassie. Be a good girl and do as you're told.'

I didn't want to, but how could I have refused? I was trapped. We were rushing towards something new, unexplored, incomprehensible. It was like watching the view from a moving train, seeing everything without quite being a part of it. The room was still except for the crackle of the fire. Binky was staring at me, willing me on. Our eyes met, and as I slipped the button in my waistband from its place, I felt a rush of wind as I went spiralling down, down, down into nothingness. I pulled at the zip, shuffled my jeans over my bottom, and eased them down over my knees.

'You should lend your wee friend a hand, girlie,' the Laird said to Binky, and she looked back at him.

'She's my sister,' she said, and he smiled as he cast his eyes over us once more.

'Sisters,' he said. 'Of course, I knew there was something.'

'Same eyes,' said Byron.

'Aye, green as emeralds,' the Laird said. 'Come on, let's be getting a move on.'

Binky helped me keep balance as I pulled my jeans over my feet. I was wearing pink panties with tulips embroidered in the elastic, flimsy and feminine. They seemed to hold great interest for the Laird and he studied the swell of my pubis for a long time before turning again to Binky.

'You did that very well, lassie, very well. Now, help your sister, do this last teeny wee thing for me.'

The horror of what he was suggesting made the breath catch in my throat. Up until then it had seemed almost innocent. He was punishing us for damaging his property. We were a couple of city girls, and he was a hill farmer making fun of us. I'd thought about old Mrs. McTavish making dinner in the kitchen and had felt safe with her there. Binky was trembling, unable to speak.

'Don't,' I said, my voice a whisper.

He turned from Binky to me, his blue eyes like fire. He was about to speak, but took a great gasp of air and, in one movement, his left hand was around my back, and with his right he grabbed the front of my knickers and pulled them down to my feet. The breath went out of me. I was naked. Completely naked. My armpits were damp, my breasts were swollen and my nipples really hurt.

'There now,' he said, as if something had been proved, and folded his arms.

What self-respect I had left disappeared as Byron slipped my knickers over my feet and stood, staring into the gusset. I knew they were sticky and felt so ashamed as he held the damp strip of cotton under his nose. When Jean-Luc Cartier had sniffed at my knickers in his office I had been mortified and imagined only a Frenchmen would have such a sordid fascination with girls' underwear. I was wrong, obviously. Byron seemed transfixed by my soiled pants and looked as if he might stand there all night inspecting the pale yellow stain.

'Well, have you finished, mon?'

'I'm just checking.'

'So I see,' said the Laird, and turned to Binky.

In the same way that she had not been told to remove her bra before she did so, she hooked her thumbs in the elastic of her white panties and wriggled them delicately down her legs. The Laird held out his hand, and the triangle of cotton looked like the head of an orchid stretched across his palm. He gave her warm knickers to Byron, who again gazed lewdly in the gusset before running the fabric under his nose. The Laird watched impatiently.

'Well?' he asked.

'Ripe, I'd say, Hamish.'

The Laird nodded sagely before turning to Binky. 'You're a good girl,' he said, and glanced back at me.

He made me feel as if I were the bad girl. He had blamed me for breaking the padlock, for soiling his fresh hay. I was utterly exposed, humiliated. I was shaking, my breasts hurt, and I know hindsight is all very well, but I had known when I had taken that first sip of buck's fizz at the *King's Head* that Binky was going to get me into trouble.

'Now, what do you think of this, Byron McBride. Has a more pretty sight ever crossed those wretched eye balls of yours?'

'Not in this lifetime, Hamish. It's a rare and lovely sight, a rare and lovely sight indeed.'

'Aye, and what are we going to do to punish these defiant Jezebels?'

'It's not for me to say. It's for me to obey.'

'Ah, it must be the muse that's brought the poetry out in you, laddie.'

They were gazing at us in wonder. At our pert breasts and lush pussies, our tiny waists and thin shoulders. I suppose we had never looked better and there was some youthful arrogance in the way I kept my back straight, my chin high. There was fear in me, shame, too, but also a weird inexplicable excitement.

I glanced towards the uncurtained windows, as if someone might be passing, not that anyone would ever pass that house. The sky was black. The storm had moved on and a sprinkling of stars had come out. Orange flames floated across the grate like dancers and the Laird's blue eyes were the eyes of a serpent, drawing me back, holding me in their power. I was naked, utterly exposed, my breasts tingling, my tummy filled with butterflies. My breath came in hot rushes and I realized I was panting.

Binky was staring at me. The Laird took her hand, directing it to the base of my spine. Our hips crossed, locking together, and I turned nervously as she began to stroke the soft flesh of my bottom, over the sloping hill to the undercurve and back again, her caress warming the moisture inside me, and I felt a dampness like dew on the lips of my vagina. The beautiful woman in the painting above the fire was staring down with a knowing expression, her dark eyes full of sadness and secrets.

In the darkness the two men had become shadows. It felt as if we were alone, two naked girls discovering something that had been hidden, our bodies drawn naturally, subconsciously together. Our breasts touched and my nipples burned like the fire in the grate. Binky's eyes flickered and closed. She had thrown back her head, presenting her long neck, which I kissed, softly biting the ivory skin, her hand on my bottom running up my back to the nape of my neck.

I circled her waist. I ran my tongue over her neck, her chin, into her mouth, her plump lips sucking at my lips, and I thought back to that first fleeting peck as we'd entered the barn. I had never kissed my sister before and it was exquisite, her soft tongue circling my tongue, our engorged lips sliding into new positions, pushing greedily as if we were devouring some rare gorgeous feast.

Our pubic mounts were touching and we swiveled our hips, grinding the bones together. I ran my hand over Binky's back. I had never appreciated how slight and fragile she was, her narrow waist widening over slender hips, her spine that I now traversed, up over the well-defined little nubs and down to the hollows in the small of her back. Her thin body relaxed as if it were a bow string too tightly wound. Her bottom was soft, round, springy, and I felt a syrupy ooze between her cheeks. Binky's hand made the same journey, over my back, then through the crack in my bottom where she found the same oily wetness, the smell of our arousal so rich and shocking it took my breath away. We were the same height, the same size, and it was like touching yourself, like masturbating.

When the Laird's big hands rested in the middle of our shoulders, one on each side, the mood was disturbed, the passion drifting away like the swell of the tide retreating back to sea.

'Shush, now, shush. Be still.'

His voice was a chant and when we realized what was happening it was already too late. Byron was on his knees attaching leather straps to our ankles, binding us together. We struggled, but the Laird's hand's pressed like the jaws of a vice and we were paralysed. Byron strapped our wrists, swiftly, with skilful fingers, right to left, and we had to widen our legs to keep balance.

The Laird still kept his hands on our backs. I looked up to plead with him but his eyes were glazed. He was staring across the room at the portrait of the lady and I imagined with a sick feeling the long history of debauchery that haunted this secluded manor house.

Byron dragged a heavy dining chair towards us and the Laird stepped up on the red upholstered seat. Immediately above on the beam were two hooks. Byron passed the Laird two lengths of leather which he attached. He reached down for our bound wrists, the swivel join between the straps allowing him to hoist our arms above our heads. He connected our wrists to the straps, first one side, then the other. We struggled, even though it was pointless. Byron was holding Binky because she looked as if she were ready to faint, and though I squirmed and screamed, I couldn't move, and there was no one to hear me. The Laird tightened the straps in such a way that our feet only just touched the ground.

How did this happen? Did we bring it upon ourselves? We had taken our clothes off, not willingly, but we hadn't put up that much of a fight. I had stood there proud of my full breasts and firm pink nipples. Binky, too, she was just the same, her silky white body displayed so shamelessly in the firelight. While the Laird had been testing us, I'd thought I'd been testing him.

He stood down, stroking our damp flesh, a potter making a vase, over our backs and around the swell of our backsides. There is nothing more humiliating than to bind two girls in this way, and the Laird was aware of his masterwork as he paused to study us, our arms stretched above our heads, our stomachs pulled in, our bottoms thrust out. We were exposed and vulnerable in every way.

It was the most degrading thing that had ever happened to me and yet, and yet, there was a part of me that wanted to know what was going to happen next. What could happen next? I'm not sure why, but I kissed Binky. Not long and luxuriously, like before, just a kiss to say it was all right. We would get through this. Tears rolled down her cheeks, one after the other, and I licked them away. Byron moved the chair back to its place at the table. The Laird circled us.

'Two wee sisters,' he said, a tone of awe in his voice. 'Now, girls, I want you to scream as loud and as long as you can. Do it for an old hill farmer, just to bring a bit of pleasure into my life.'

I lifted my head and stared at him, made him focus. 'What are you going to do?' I demanded.

'I'm going to give you want you need, girlie.'

He clicked his fingers and Byron went to the walnut dresser against the wall. He opened the top drawer, removed something, and closed the drawer again. He returned and placed across the Laird's two outstretched palms a leather riding crop with an ornamental tassel.

'I'm going to thrash you, lassie. That round bottom you keep pushing oot is going to be tanned until its raw.'

I don't know where I got the courage from, but I spat in his face, an enormous mouthful of spittle that drooled down into his red beard. He grinned and clucked me tenderly under the chin. 'That's what I like to see, Byron. A bit of spunk.'

As he spoke, he slid the riding crop through the cheeks of my bottom and up, first between my legs, then Binky's legs, locked against my own. He bowed the crop as if playing a cello, slowly, gently, backwards and forwards, and the breath caught in my throat. I sucked at the air and felt a deep raging shame as the liquids leaked from me, wetting my thighs. He kept sliding the crop back and forth, back and forth, urging little gasps from my throat, the crop so soft and the sawing motion so mesmerizing, without thinking, I dragged down on the straps and rolled my pelvis until the wings of my pussy opened.

When the Laird slid the crop out and showed it to Byron, I saw that it was sticky, slicked and shiny with juice. Why were we wet like this? We should have been dry with shame, but my sister's naked body pressed tightly to me was intensely erotic, the prurient gaze of the two men so decadent, my embarrassment was submerged by my arousal.

Laird ran his finger along the length of the soggy crop, then leaned over me, tickling my bottom playfully with the tassel. 'There, you see, lassie,' he said. 'You're going to enjoy this.'

He was close enough for me to spit again but I didn't. I'd made my point. I kept my dignity. He gave Byron the riding crop and the two men stood back, one on each side of us, our bodies in profile, and although I knew what was about to happen, it still seemed unreal, unbelievable.

'Are you ready, lad?'

'Aye, Hamish, as ready as I'll ever be.'

'Together then.'

There was no pause. Byron brought the crop down on my bottom, a swift, hard slash that cut across my pale skin, and the pain that roared through me was like no pain I had ever felt before, a sting, a burn with acid, a flash of fire. Yet even while I was absorbed by my pain, it was the sound of the Laird's big hand slapping Binky that resounded in my ears. She screamed so loudly, and was so close, it felt as if the scream came from my own lungs.

We rolled with the blow and as I watched the Laird draw back his hand, I knew that behind me, Byron McBride was lifting the riding crop. Down it came again, another flash of lightening, just above the first, cutting deep, searing my skin. Tears were gushing from my eyes. My back was drenched and Binky pressed against me felt as if she were on fire.

The next strike with the crop was lower, making a pattern, the line nearer to my sex. My vagina was shamefully engorged, pouting lasciviously between my thighs. Binky was sobbing against my neck, and I wanted to stroke her hair, comfort her, but our arms were pulled above our heads and the only comfort I could give was to kiss her ear.

The riding crop came down again like a whiplash, the sound of the Laird's big hand spanking Binky's bottom like a clap of thunder that echoed and vibrated around the room. She didn't scream now. She just sobbed, her body trembling. Each new stroke of the riding crop was as painful as the last, but pain changes in character, and when you are familiar with pain, it doesn't seem quite so terrible.

Byron left six strokes on my backside, six red lines of burning agony, the fire in each stripe warming the whole area, up my back to my neck, down my thighs to my feet. My posterior was a furnace, my front was running with the sweat pouring from our two naked bodies, and as I stood there, arms suspended above my head, I felt like a diver at the end of the high diving board, the void stretched out below me. Something had crossed over in me. I had changed. I had become under the beating a new person, more aware of my senses, more conscious of my own desires.

The Laird bent to inspect Binky's bottom. Now that it had become pitch black outside, the long windows were a wall of mirrors and I could see his reflection, this giant of a man bending over the thin elongated body of my sister, his big fingers pressing tentatively at her bottom as if it were a rare delicate fruit he was about to consume. Byron was inspecting my raw buttocks in the same way, then joined the Laird before they traded positions. Byron flexed his muscles, smiting the air with a test stroke, his eyes meeting mine.

'Now, are you ready, laddie?' the Laird asked.

Byron smiled. 'Aye, ready and willing,' he replied.

He raised the crop, and as he brought it down on Binky's hind quarters, I felt the terrible smack of the Laird's hand on my own. Binky was thrust against me, our dank bodies slippery as fish, like two slimy creatures mysteriously mating. The pleasure and the pain were two threads woven together, making both stronger, more powerful. Before I could catch my breath, the second spank was scolding my flesh, the Laird's huge hand covering the entire surface of my bottom, the sting making the six stripes left by the crop blaze more brightly.

Binky was alternatively sobbing and screaming. I tried not to weep, but the Laird's will was stronger and I couldn't stop myself. It was what he expected, what he wanted. We had done everything he wanted. My body was numb. The fire in my raw bottom was growing calmer and, as the third smack found its mark, I hardly felt it at all. All I could feel was Binky pressed against me, our breasts so hot and wet, our pubic mounts slapping urgently together.

As the fourth smack made contact with my bottom, I didn't cry, and I didn't scream. I found Binky's lips and kissed her. She was surprised at first, but pushed back, sucking at my lips, running her tongue over my teeth, curling the trunk in little twirls down my throat. The two men pumped themselves up, readying themselves for the fifth stroke, and as I saw Byron's arm come down, I felt my stomach clench with contractions.

There was no breath in my body. I was a balloon emptied of gas. I gasped and panted. My mouth had fallen open. I pushed my bottom out to meet the Laird's hand, the muscles of my stomach tightened, and a spasm gripped my pussy. I was desperate with desire, aching with dirty, immodest needs. I could smell my fruity arousal. Or was it Binky's arousal? We were pressed so close I couldn't tell, and the air I breathed was charged on pure unadulterated sex.

Take me. Take me. Take me.

The words ran through my head and just thinking them made me feel carnal, defiled, promiscuous. I was eighteen. A virgin still. And I wanted the Laird to take me, take me now while the liquids were hot between my legs. I watched and I waited. Byron raised his arm one last time and I gazed at him, eyes wide, knowing that as the riding crop beat the small drum of Binky's bottom, the Laird's brutish palm would crash like a ringing cymbal across my bruised beaten flesh, the pain mingling with a crude pleasure that had begun to release the creamy juices brewing inside me.

He put more effort into that last grand wallop and I roared like a wounded beast as the Laird's hand tattooed its shape on my bottom. I was shaking, trembling, forcing my pubic bone into Binky's open legs, wailing frenziedly, and trying to reach for something just beyond my grasp. The chastisement was over but unfinished, incomplete.

The Laird was retrieving the chair. Byron was already unbuckling the straps around our ankles. I looked into Binky's eyes. They were glossed with tears and exhilaration. I could smell the piquant aromas wafting from her groin and soft white armpits. It made my head spin. The Laird untied the straps holding our arms.

'Get the carpet for the girlies, what are you waiting for laddie?' he said, and Byron took the fleece from the fireside and placed it at our feet.

My arms hurt. We had been standing on our toes for so long, we collapsed on the soft pile of the fleece, our slippery soaked bodies coiling together. I reached for Binky's breast, popped the hard mount in my mouth, and bit down on the bud until she squealed. She did the same to me, and the agony was excruciating, so intense fresh tears stung my eyes. I bit her neck. I licked the entire surface of her ear, and we kissed with some unimaginable yearning. I was grunting, sucking at the air, my body turning instinctively, driven by the pull of the moon, by some alien lust.

As I moved my tongue down between Binky's breasts, she did the same to me. I supped at the tiny cup of her belly button, and down into the sopping pink gash between her legs.

Her puffy lips opened and her taste on my tongue was fresh and bittersweet. It was the taste of a girl, my own little sister, something new to me, divine, something to savour. Her clever tongue was exploring the cavern of my sex, pushing in and out, in and out, and I did the same, bathing my face in her smell, gorging on her lush creamy juice, oblivious to everything except Binky's hot oozing pussy.

I wasn't even aware of the two men standing above us, gazing down as if at animals in the zoo, two naked creatures with spanked bottoms slurping at each other's most intimate places. There had been knots inside my tummy ever since we had arrived at the manor house, and those knots were undoing, smoothing out, caressing me like tiny hands, the feeling of relief spreading like nectar down my throat, through my breasts, my organs, my flaming insides. I gripped Binky's soft thighs in my palms and lapped at her, her thick creamy girl juice sticky and warm on my face.

Binky's tongue was nursing the glowing nib of my clitoris. I did the same for her. We were *yin* and *yang*, blonde and dark, four emerald eyes. The spasms running through me were running through her. A sprinkle of pre-orgasm fluids soft as raindrops touched my tongue. Binky lifted her bottom up from the fleece, and as she started to come, my own orgasm broke from me like a fizzing firework, a beating pulse of pure energy that reverberated through my body. Never, never, had had anything like this happened to me before, and I pressed my sex into Binky until I had emptied every last drop of hot fluid into her throat.

I gasped for air, then ran my tongue through the crack in her bottom, into the dark winking eyelet throbbing restlessly, wetly above, tasting her, wanting every part of her, giving every part of myself to her. Had we always wanted this? Had the Laird found something so secret in us we didn't even know ourselves?

The thought had come and gone again. I felt Binky's little tongue wriggle into my bottom, the pressure reaching my swollen clitoris, and I started to come again, the pitch softer, the energy spent, a feeling like the last glow of the setting sun.

I was sopping and delirious, too exhausted to struggle as the Laird suddenly, unexpectedly lifted me from Binky in his big hands and carried me limply to the table. He placed me at the far end, away from the plates and silverware set for three, and I lay there exhausted.

'There, lassie, there,' he whispered.

Byron pulled at Binky's hand; she came unsteadily to her feet. He placed her opposite me across the width of the table, the expanse of polished walnut so wide between us, when they again connected the bindings at our wrists, our arms were stretched out, my torso resting on the tabletop in such a way that my spanked bottom was forced up in the air.

'Together, then,' said the Laird.

I watched as Byron pushed his sporran to one side. He tucked the hem of his kilt in the waistband, and from out of the darkness revealed his erect penis. He eased Binky's legs apart, and at the same moment, I felt my own legs being opened, the ricochet effect obscene and inexplicably carnal. As Byron slid his cock into Binky, the Laird's cock ran up my thighs until the head rested against the entrance to my vagina. It was huge, and as it pushed patiently through my drenched lips, the walls of my hot pussy were expanding and contracting, pushing back, the giant cock greased by my orgasm sliding slowly, inevitably, like a landslide up inside me, breaking my hymen. I'd finally lost my virginity and it was a little thrill that the Laird didn't even know.

My mouth fell open. I closed my eyes. I was a woman. I was making love, and it was like nothing I'd ever known before because I'd never done it before. My hips bucked and rolled. I pushed back, thrusting out my thrashed bottom, absorbing every inch of the monster. I was impaled, skewered, his big balls like church bells chiming mutely against my thighs, his coarse hair chafing my soft skin as he rammed into me harder and harder, faster and faster.

It grew more intense, more ferocious. He held me in one big hand and with the other started slapping my hips and sides as if urging a race horse to take a high fence, and I took the fence, and the next one, pushing back against the Laird and taking everything he had to give.

He started to groan, his voice emerging from far away, from deep down in the depths of his immense body. He was vanishing inside me, withdrawing almost entirely, then plunging back between the drenched walls of my pussy with great ardent thrusts, my thighs locked, my back arched in a bow, my arms stretched out until both Binky and I rose clean off the table and I felt like a bird flying through the air. I was being split apart like a length of wood, the Laird's cock a sharpened axe, and then he exploded, roaring, pumping into me, and his semen was an endless gush like oil from a well, like lava from an erupting volcano, like a tidal wave, like a soft warm sea.

Byron was mutely wailing in the background. So was Binky. So was I. I was climaxing again, my body hollowed out. The contractions felt as if I were giving birth, and I was, to a new part of myself, to my future. The Laird kept pumping away, but already he was growing softer and already I sensed a woeful absence as his giant penis slipped from me on a torrent of steaming sperm. I could smell it, rich like fresh milk, thick as cream.

Now that it was over, I felt drained and, I had to admit, indecently satisfied. Binky was panting, her eyes staring without seeing, her cheek resting on the tabletop, the ridge of her bottom rising and falling. My ribs were bruised. My breasts hurt. The lips of my pussy were opening and closing, quivering like a sea anemone as the Laird's sperm oozed from me like syrup in bubbling slurps, vulgar and sensuous. The Laird caught his breath. He gave my backside a playful slap.

'You're a good girl, lassie,' he said and, absurdly, I felt proud.

Byron straightened his kilt, then released the bindings at our wrists. We slid apart and I came shakily to my feet. The Laird took me by the arms and stared into my eyes.

'Now, is that better?' he asked seriously, and I bit my lips and nodded.

Binky was still lying across the table, the tips of her toes just touching the floor. Byron was examining her, and when the Laird joined him, I followed, the sap and semen turning cold as it trickled down the insides of my legs.

Binky's swollen vulva was pressed between her thighs and Byron's emissions put a gloss over the inflamed pattern that covered the entire surface of her bottom. I stared and it was hard to turn my head away. I was transfixed, mesmerized. Binky's bottom was fiery red, glowing like the flames in the fire, the six livid stripes from the crop the same African violet as the trim on Binky's pink car: the same colour as the lines running down the Laird's kilt.

My mouth dropped open. My heart skipped. I stared at his kilt, then up into his eyes. He smiled, nodding his head warmly.

'Aye, lassie,' he said. 'You're a clever girl.'

I ran my palm softly over Binky's bottom, and looked back again at the Laird.

'It's my clan: the tartan plaid of the Black Watch.'

Binky had finally caught her breath. I put my arms around her waist as she slipped to her feet. The Laird crossed the room to the piano, grabbed the carved stool, and placed it at the end of the table facing the place settings at the far end.

'You can sit here, lassies, you must be famished,' the Laird said, and I felt grateful for his kindness. He turned to Byron, waving his hand towards the fire. 'Do you think we live in a barn, laddie, all this stuff hanging aboot. Put it away, for heaven's sake, mon.'

I watched without fully taking in what was happening as Byron gathered our damp clothing. My heart was pounding, and only slowly did I become conscious of us sitting there naked, my breasts throbbing, my nipples still erect, Binky holding my hand like a lost girl. My bottom stung, but all my senses were so alive, the sting was more pleasure than pain. The Laird found a piece of cloth in the chest beside the fire. He gazed up at the portrait of the woman, turned momentarily to me, then turned his attention to the shiny wet discharges we'd deposited on the table.

'Here, lassie, look at the mess you've made,' he said, and obediently I polished the puddles of sperm from the table.

I had just finished the task when the door opened. Byron returned pushing an old-fashioned serving trolley, the wheels squeaking. Mrs. McTavish carried two bowls and soupspoons; she was sucking at her gums and tutting to herself. She set the bowls down in front of us. Byron placed an enormous tureen in front the Laird and Mrs. McTavish served three plates of stew. She glanced in our direction as she sat opposite Byron. The Laird was between them at the head of the table.

'Come on then, eat if you're going to,' he said.

We ladled soup into our bowls, filling them to the brim. The steam was hot and the smell was delicious. We sat and ate like two little animals. Soup dribbled from my mouth, down my chin and fell, burning my breast. As I wiped the drips away with my hand, the Laird caught my eye and smiled.

'Tell me, Mrs. McTavish, have you ever seen finer titties?'

'What are you talking about, mon?'

'Look at them, bright as wee buttons.'

'You're disgusting,' she said, and the Laird grinned as he ate his soup.

His eyes were flicking constantly from the bowl in front of him to the two of us, squeezed together on the stool like ornaments on a shelf. I tried to picture us both in the Laird's eyes, two naked girls like two little animals, our breasts perky, our cheeks and eyes bright, our bodies electric with life, with new sensations.

It was only as I filled my tummy and my heart began to beat more normally that I became aware that our clothes had been taken away. I gazed back along the table at the Laird.

He nodded.

'Aye, lassie,' he said. 'You can bed down in the woodshed. If you piddle in the straw like wee animals you cannae expect a bed to sleep in.'

'What about our clothes?'

'You won't be needing those. Not tonight.'

Binky looked at me for an explanation but there wasn't one. I looked back at the Laird and felt a warm dribble leak on his piano stool.

Reviews For Being A Girl

"…the bible of new erotica."
D. LUCIUS RHINEHART, AMAZON.COM

"... a well written novel with copious amounts of eroticism to keep the fires burning in more places than one. I look forward to future offerings from this feisty author."
CARRIE WHITE, INK'S EROTICA

"This simply is a joyous and wonderful read, from someone who clearly has been to the edges of reality, taken a knife from their pocket, cut through and stepped beyond. There is a feeling of confession, of wanting to understand more, explore further and see where you can push.

"Some of the moments, in another novel might feel contrived, but here they are held together by an honesty and fresh exploration. Maturity is waiting in the wings. Reading this book makes you want to do the same, and I am expecting greater words from this writer. Finally. Can I have my own Milly."
PHAEDRUS, AMAZON.CO.UK

In the second extract taken from *A Girl's Adventure,* published by the Accent Press Xcite imprint in 2010, failed actress Greta May learns obedience. Richard, her new Master, is a Pony Girl enthusiast and is beginning to take Greta through her paces.

Back-cover blub:

> *When a mysterious stranger gives failed actress Greta May his phone number, she dreams of adventure and plucks up the courage to call him. But the moment she enters his flat he rips off her knickers and spanks her bottom. At first shocked and humiliated, Greta grows bewildered as the pain turns to pleasure, and after being tied to the bed for a thrashing, she agrees with rising excitement to play a game where she will win a prize if she does everything Richard demands.*

> *It is the beginning of an erotic journey of self-discovery, where Greta meets Dirty Bill, the water sports specialist; Vanlooch, who uses oils from unusual places to highlight his portraits, and the moody Count Ruspoli who, after bedding 10,000 women, has taken a vow of chastity. Can Greta save him? Under Richard's firm hand Greta finds her true nature through discipline and, after meeting film director and bogwash artiste Tyler Copic, she seizes the elusive prize: the chance to play the role that will change her life and put her back in the spotlight.*

The Game

In the cab taking them to Camden Market the driver had already admitted that he was *infatuated* with Margaret Thatcher and was now drawing an improbable connection between rude cyclists and failings in education.

'Bring back the bloody birch,' he hissed in well-oiled alliteration.

91

Richard made informed comments but she could tell that he had no interest in politics at all. She had no idea what interested Richard - well, that's not true, she had an inkling; she had six perfectly spaced pink lines across her bottom and a feeling that she was finding the role nature had craftily intended.

Strangers on a train. She had never done *anything* like this before and it was liberating. She had hungered for adventure. That's why she had left her friends behind and gone to drama school in the first place. Acting had been her passion since she was little but it did grow tiresome always being type cast.

When she looked at herself in the mirror she saw clear, sparkling green eyes, a wide mouth with sulky full lips and neat features framed by a curtain of chestnut brown hair, a shoe-in for *A Midsummer's Night Dream*. She had, full dome-shaped breasts (designed for lap-dancing!), wide shoulders, long slender legs and a little tummy that pouted in a saucy curve.

It must have been the mirror's cruel trickery that in her reflection Greta perceived the leading lady while the casting agents and directors saw the girl who is forever being slapped and smacked and tied in chains. She had never quite understood why and appreciated now that those agents and directors had been rather more astute than she'd cared to realise.

She flicked through *The Stage* Richard had brought back with the pizza. There was simply nothing for leading ladies! It was amusing for a moment to consider giving Jason Wise a call. After all, her old boyfriend had only craved what Richard had roundly taken. A buzz zinged through her as she pictured herself being lashed to his bed, her bottom mooning up to meet his belt, her silky flesh being thrashed.

I've been thrashed and buggered. Well and truly buggered. She just adored this word. It rolled off the tongue. It was like smack. I've been smacked and buggered. Buggered and smacked. Gagged and hooded, stretched like a starfish and taken a big throbbing cock deep into my cute little ass. Mmm.

She wriggled and leaked and remembered she wasn't wearing any panties.

Now, what was she thinking about?

Oh, yes. Jason Wise. Jason who was all mouth and trousers, or a lack of them, all promises that never came to pass, the part that never happened, the LA director who never appeared. He was the dust on a bookshelf, a relic from the past best left undisturbed. To escape his clutches she had left working in theatre but it was only temporary. On a journey it is the diversions that make life interesting.

Greta turned to look out the taxi window. The sun was putting a sheen on the shop windows and she had an intuition that the drive across London was taking her into the future, not to a minor role, but something bigger, more important, that everything until that moment had just been a rehearsal.

The road was bumpy. She bobbed up and down, the slaps against her buttocks giving her the same warm coddled feeling that she'd had when she sank into Richard's blue bath. He held her still, his calming hand moving up her thigh and she felt her blood grow warm, the breath catch in her throat. She was leaking still and the pungent aroma that rose from under the hem of her black dress made her blush. She slid forward as his hand vanished into the valley between her legs. A finger parted her labia, stroking the swollen petals in a beckoning motion, and she was disappointed when his mobile buzzed and he pulled away to answer.

'Gustav,' he said brightly. 'You're in town?'

Pause. For some reason, Greta was holding her breath.

'Listen, I have found something with a *lot* of potential.'

Pause. He was rolling the goo between his thumb and first finger like a gardener with the earth. She was fertile soil waiting to be ploughed and sown.

'Young. A bit ungainly, you know, the usual.'

Pause.

'They always need training, Gustav. This one's a quick learner.'

It sounded to Greta as if they were talking about a race horse and she thought Richard was probably a trainer and spent a lot of time outdoors; he had a sun tan already and it was only June. While he was listening, he slid his sticky finger into her mouth and the taxi driver was watching in the rear view mirror as she sucked it.

'…okay, we'll be at the gallery,' Richard said finally and glanced at his watch. 'Say twelve o'clock.' He paused again. 'Yes, that's an idea. Bring it along.'

He closed the phone and turned to her. 'Good,' he added with a thoughtful expression.

'Who was that?' she asked.

He narrowed his eyes and rubbed the end of her nose with his wet finger. 'Let's play a game,' he suggested. 'It's fun.'

'I like games,' she said and really meant it.

'Okay. Listen very carefully: you must do everything – everything I say. And not ask why.'

'That doesn't sound like much of a game to me.'

'But there's a prize.'

Her eyes brightened. 'What?'

'You mustn't ask,' he said.

'Meany.'

'Or it won't be a surprise.'

She tapped her bottom lip with a finger. 'But what if it's not a very good prize?' she asked.

'The best prizes are like unicorns. They don't appear unless you believe in them.'

That didn't make much sense to Greta so she just shrugged.

'A deal?' he asked.

She pretended to think about it but she had already made up her mind. 'A deal,' she replied and they shook hands.

The streets were crowded as they stepped out of the cab. The sunshine was warm on her bare shoulders and the air smelled of ripe peaches. Richard reached urgently for her wrist and dragged her in a mad dash to the last available table at the street café on the corner beating two other couples in the process.

'You're quick,' she said breathlessly.

'You've got to grab *every* opportunity,' he told her. 'Grab it and hold on tight.' He was holding her two hands across the table, he squeezed hard, then let go to snap his fingers for the waiter.

The morning croissants had been tipped down the waste grinder and Greta was starving. She reached for the menu, wincing as she changed positions on the metal chair, a blush coloring her cheeks and neck. She was learning new things about herself and knew that of all knowledge it is self-knowledge that matters most. If she were cast now in *Mcbeth* or *Titus Andronicus* she would willingly submit her flesh to the ravages of madmen. She admired excess in others and was discovering an untapped well of excess in herself. She even liked the word excess. It was like sex only backwards.

Richard ordered a full English breakfast.

She looked up from the menu. 'I'll have the same.'

The waiter ignored her and Richard glanced at her with raised eye-brows as he continued the order. 'And the lady will have the wild oats with strawberries.' *Oats*, she was thinking, as the waiter wrote it down. 'Two fresh orange juices and a double espresso.'

We're already playing the game, she realised. 'You can never be too rich or too thin,' she said with sarcasm when the waiter had gone.

'Or too obedient,' Richard added.

Then he smiled and it occurred to her that she liked this game, whatever the prize. She was going to ask Richard if he trained race horses but it was more fun not knowing anything, his job, his surname, his hobbies.

She focused on his blue eyes. 'People hate being looked at on the tube,' she remarked.

'Not everyone.'

'Everyone,' she said emphatically. 'How many girls have you given your number to?'

'Very few as it happens.'

'I bet that's not true.'

'They are always *very* carefully selected.'

She didn't really believe him but was pleased anyway. 'I was chosen?' she asked.

He tapped the end of her nose. 'Questions. Questions. Questions,' he said, and he wasn't smiling.

She tucked into her oats and strawberries. It was surprisingly good and it seemed as if even her taste buds had had awoken like Snow White after a long interminable sleep. She glanced up. He was studying her, watching her lips.

'Selected,' she said, and he wiped milk from the corners of her mouth. 'Even I didn't know I was going to call you.'

'Saturday evening and you're looking at the TV listings in the paper.'

'All the boys my age are so boring.'

'You're…twenty?'

'Almost.'

'What kind of school did you go to?'

I didn't answer.

'A boarding school. A convent,' he suggested and she frowned because he was right. 'With nasty little nuns.'

'Vicious, actually.'

'You miss the discipline, Greta May,' he said. 'It is the secret of being a great actress.'

'That's what they said at drama school.'

'And they were right.'

He carried on eating and Greta thought back to the brief conversation when she was in the bath; she'd had a feeling as Richard was leaving to get the pizzas that he knew exactly who she was, that they weren't strangers who had met by chance on a train. She'd thought it then and she thought it now. She had been selected, as he put it, chosen for a role and, if that were so, she intended to give the best performance of her life.

She wriggled in her chair and the lightning flash across the marks of discipline made her wriggle even more.

The two couples they had beaten to the table were still waiting, each glaring at their partner, blaming them for the delay, and when she thought back to those months when she'd lived with Jason what had lodged in her memory was the pettiness of it all, his reprimands *to make her better*, his smelly socks, the sink full of saucepans and grey stubble in her tooth brush.

a relationship there is always tension but with a stranger all those pressures are forgotten and you can just give in to your fantasies. Her mind stretched back over the three years since she'd left school and what she recalled most was doing things she didn't really want to be doing, learning her craft with dull repetition, reading for parts that rarely came, the incessant ennui. She wasn't exactly sure what ennui meant but it was from a play by someone wicked like Jean Genet or Guy de Maupassant and she knew it was something intolerable.

Richard stirred his espresso.

'Why didn't you get me one?'

He didn't reply and she remembered she wasn't supposed to ask.

'Coffee bleaches the calcium from young bones,' he then said.

'What about my cigarettes?' she asked hopefully.

'Ah, yes.' He had insisted that she leave her bag at his flat, she didn't need money or her mobile phone, he explained, and carried her *Camels* in his pocket. He gave them to her and she slipped one between her pouty lips. It waggled as she spoke.

'Do you have my lighter?'

He took it from his pocket and held it up between two fingers, but instead of giving it to her, he pushed the ashtray across the table. 'Take the cigarette out of your mouth and break it into small pieces.'

The cigarette froze.

'What?'

'I don't need to repeat myself, do I, Greta?'

The game, she thought, and reluctantly did as she was told, breaking the back of the *Camel* and discarding it.

'Now take them all out of the packet, one at a time, and break them into the ashtray.'

She sniffed haughtily but it was for her own good she realised and obeyed his instructions. He watched the pile of ruined cigarettes fill the ashtray and then crushed the empty packet.

'Smoking is strictly against the rules,' he said.

'I didn't know there were other rules as well.'

'Then you must learn, mustn't you,' he said firmly and she nodded tamely because she knew he was right. Richard pushed the ashtray to one side. 'Come on,' he added, 'you need a new dress. That's for evenings.'

He paid the bill and the girls who had been waiting for the table gave her a dirty look as they passed. Richard took her hand as if it were a part of him and they crossed the road to wander among stalls of glittery tops and turquoise jewellery, healing crystals and flak jackets. She slowed to watch a cartoonist drawing sketches but Richard tugged on her hand

and she trotted along like a pony, clip-clopping in her backless black suede shoes behind him.

She could smell Indian spices and ice cream, the sharp tang of petrol as the fire-eater blew streams of flame from his blackened lips. Richard tossed her lighter into his hat. Everything was going, going, going. She had left *The Stage* on the table at the restaurant. She didn't need to search for a part. She already had her role.

Boys were taking off their tee-shirts and tucking them into the backs of their jeans and girls were wearing less and less and she thought one day a clever designer would come up with the ultimate design and dress them in nothing at all.

As they moved into the heart of the market the crowd was more dense and people were staring at her as if they knew her from somewhere but couldn't quite recall where. It puzzled Greta that she was getting so much attention and decided not to think about it and just enjoy it. She was seeing herself as if from outside herself, her aura faintly glowing. Like her bottom.

She gave it a little wiggle and at that moment her line of vision was struck by a sulky brunette in a silver dress, her body moving amorphously, her velvet eyes as she lowered her dark glasses full of energy and secrets. She ran her tongue over her lips and there was something carnal in the way she slid her fingers across Greta's bare arm as they crossed.

Greta straightened her shoulders and swung her hips. Richard was still holding her hand when they stumbled upon the perfect stall where white cotton dresses swayed above on a line like clouds in the breeze. They went through the rail and Richard found a Little Miss Muffet outfit with puffy sleeves and a high neck. It was truly awful. She pulled a face and then shrugged when his stern look reminded Greta there was a prize at stake.

'You have to try it on.'

'What?' she said. She couldn't believe it...

'Here,' he said emphatically.

'Richard…'

He folded his arms.

'Don't you remember,' she whispered, 'you ripped my knickers off. I'm not wearing anything.'

He held up his palm as if it were a paddle and showed how it could be put to good use. Greta looked around her.

'There are like…loads of people.'

Sweat prickled her armpits. Her cheeks coloured. He wanted to see her naked in the busy market and the scary thought struck her that she wanted it too. She had a craving like thirst or hunger – or for nicotine - an irrepressible desire to expose her breasts that tingled, her moist pussy, her bottom with its pink stripes like a badge of obedience and humiliation. She wanted to take her clothes off in the market place just as she had done all those years ago in the garden.

Richard was staring into her eyes as she reached for the thin black straps and slid them one at a time over her shoulders. She hesitated. There were corrugations on his brow, a look of impatience about his lips. She continued, peeling the material from her breasts. She paused for just a second, pulled at the tie and let the dress fall shimmering about her ankles.

As Greta stepped away from the black pool of material she was overcome by a surge of contentment. The tingle that crossed her bottom as it was exposed to the air tempted a squirt of moisture from her lower lips and her flush turned crimson as she reached for the Little Miss Muffet costume. Richard was about to give it to her but suddenly changed his mind.

'No, it's not you,' he said, and gave it back to the stallholder.

Greta was so disorientated by Richard's ability to turn the normal world upside down, she hadn't noticed the stallholder trembling slightly, his mouth ajar. A crowd had gathered as if they were at a slave market in ancient Athens and a few words from a play slipped into her mind: It's not a woman's beauty that bewitches, but her nobility, a line from Euripides, and she threw back her head and stood proudly naked for everyone to see.

Richard pointed at another dress hovering above on a wire coat hanger and she'd had her eye on that one all along. The stallholder lifted it down using a hook on a long pole and she remembered the sulky-eyed brunette as the soft cotton received her curves, the bodice tight, hugging her stomach, revealing the chasm between her breasts. The skirt was embroidered in the same pattern of fleur-de-lys that decorated the ceiling in Richard's bedroom and Greta couldn't help wondering if this were more than mere chance, that the chain of events were like the links of a chain all connected and binding her to her true destiny.

As she stood straight again the silent audience spontaneously put their hands together in applause before merging back into the crowd.

'There. That wasn't difficult, was it?'

She shook her head and smoothed down the fabric.

'One day, Greta, you'll demand it.'

She wasn't exactly sure what he meant but couldn't ask. Richard considered her carefully before nodding to the stallholder. He took out his wallet and when the man folded her black dress, Richard waved it away before he could place it in a carrier bag.

'She won't be needing it,' he said, and again she bit her tongue to stop herself asking why.

Reviews for A Girl's Adventure

"...one of those cheeky, upbeat CP novels where punishment is something to be enjoyed, rather than endured. The engaging Greta quickly comes to see sex as a positive force, embracing her newfound desires with missionary (among other positions) zeal and enriching the sex lives of her friends and colleagues as she goes. You'll be left as glowing as Greta's well-spanked bottom by the end, and you'll have enjoyed the adventure."
LIZ COLDWELL – FORUM MAGAZINE

"This is a great work of the human imagination. It makes the Kama Sutra look impotent. If only there were more women like Greta! I suspect a lot of readers would like to meet Chloe too. Thurlow transmutes potential pain into pure pleasure. It is the kind of book that makes real life seem almost unbearable."
ANDY – AMAZON.CO.UK

"Oh to live the life of Greta May....If you enjoy the thought of total domination then the author of this book certainly knows how to literally push all the right buttons (excuse the pun)...

"Greta May is a beautiful young girl who has lost her way in life, a random meeting on a train change's all that in ways you could only ever imagine. The author's clever way with words draw you into Greta's life with such magnetism its hard to put the book down, but you will put the book down, probably several times, but only to release your own sexual frustrations so you can get back to concentrating on Greta's adventure.

"The characters are described so vividly you feel as though you know them and the descriptions of the various places really help you get lost inside Greta's world. You are given every saucy detail in this very raunchy read, there's a little bit of everything and I would highly recommend it to anyone."
HOUSEWIFEINTURMOIL.CO.UK

"Enticing, sexy, and just plain fun to read."
ANDREW KAISER, THE NEW NUDE MAGAZINE

The next extract is the first chapter from *The Secret Life of Girls,* published by Xcite in 2011. In this novel, Bella, the central character, is dominant and self-possessed. She thinks sex is just fun and people take it far too seriously. A virgin when the book opens, by its final page, there isn't much Bella hasn't sampled.

You may note that the erotic journey often begins with a girl having her bottom spanked. In *Shades of Grey,* EL James follows the exact same pattern.

Back-cover blurb:

> *After the gardener spanks her bottom and a nun at her elite finishing school seduces her in the catacombs, Bella realises that sex was what she was born for. She adores wearing a dildo and deflowering virgins just as much as she adores indulging the roguish Christian Thomas with his addiction to fruit salads and bondage.*
>
> *Then Bella's world comes tumbling down. She learns that her beloved Ickham Manor doesn't belong to her, it belongs to her wicked stepfather. Sex has been fun. Now it is the weapon she uses to put her world back together again. Bella entraps her stepfather in a lewd act on video. She stars in a porn flick and, as her song on the soundtrack makes her a tabloid celebrity, Bella is at the beginning of an erotic ride into the showbiz world of pain and perversion, of domination and submission.*

Wet Dream

The first time I had a wet dream was a summer night when I'd gone to bed exhausted after one of those tedious talks with Mother. Something had been welling up inside her for weeks and it had been a relief when it finally came spilling out.

'Something awful has happened, Lucy. Awful,' she said. 'I can't even tell you.'

'Mummy?'

She took a deep breath and composed her features. 'Daddy put all his money into that, that…business and…he lost it. Everything. If it wasn't for Simon I don't know what we'd do.'

Simon was Simon Daviditz and he had been a regular visitor since Daddy died. At the funeral he was holding Mother's hand but I remembered his eyes that day considering me across the grave as if I were a piece of bric-à-brac at the flea market he wasn't sure whether or not to invest in.

Mother started sniffling. 'We have to do something. We have to,' she cried. 'You won't even be able to go to your new school. It's all gone, gone.'

She dabbed her eyes repeatedly with a handkerchief while I sat there feeling cross. I was going to the finishing school of Saint Sebastian the Holy Martyr to retake my A levels and I really didn't like my plans not turning out as planned.

I left her to make her phone calls and went to bed. I fell into a deep sleep and the sun angling through the lattice windows woke me with a sense that life was starting anew and I should stop worrying about poor Daddy.

My tee-shirt was up around my neck and my hands like explorers in a foreign land were moving over my breasts, my tummy, my hips and down between my legs. It was sticky there as if honey had been spilled over my thighs and I had the odd thought that in the night someone had been packing my bags and I was about to begin a long journey.

There was a white dress draped over the chair. I pulled it over my head and slipped barefoot into the garden. Plump insects buzzed and hummed among the flowers. Red butterflies spiraled like dancers in the updrafts of air rising warmly from the lawn. The cat stopped, stared as if he'd never seen me before, then sauntered off to his place in the apple tree where he would watch for birds. Sylvester was a killer and nothing gave him more pleasure than dragging wriggling, half-expired game into the kitchen where he would display his spoils on the white tiles of the floor.

I had thought I was alone but heard Mr Lawrence softly whistling in the shed. The gardener was what Mother called a local yokel, which meant he was subnormal and she could tell unkind stories about him over the phone to her friends. I had always thought of Mr Lawrence as old and only when I entered his domain that day did I realize that he was the same age as Mr Daviditz, about forty, loads older than me, but younger than Mother.

He was preparing cuttings, trimming them with a knife with a worn shiny blade. He glanced up, nodded as he relit his roll-up, then continued whistling. In the air was the tang of cut grass, wood polish and the moth ball smell of old Jake, the Labrador, sitting immobile like a black statue beside the bench. Tools with wooden handles hung from brackets with a sense of calm and order, and ranged along the shelves were jars full of nails and screws. Through the small windows the light moved in dusty sheets and I had a feeling I was in one of those old French films Daddy would often be watching late at night when I woke from a bad dream and couldn't get back to sleep again.

My underarms were damp and perspiration rolled like glass beads over my skin. I watched absorbed as Mr Lawrence positioned the cuttings in the tray, his movements slow and steady as if he was enjoying the job and was in no hurry to get it done. He made a hole in the black earth with his thumb, selected another stem, and pressed the soil back in place. He had wide, strong fingers that fondled the fragile shoots with the same delicacy you need to sew on a button or write someone's name on a birthday cake.

He took another puff on his cigarette then left it balanced on the side of a silver tin. There was a spray gun on the bench and when all the cuttings were standing in neat lines he misted the tray with several short, sharp tugs on the trigger. I had moved closer than I meant to and the spray was cool on my hot cheeks.

For as long as I could remember, Mr Lawrence had avoided looking in my direction but now his dark eyes made me flush as they met mine. There was a faint smile on his lips as he moistened my face, my neck, and he kept on jerking the trigger on the spray gun, soaking the top of my flimsy dress. My breasts had begun to tingle and my nipples like the green shoots in the seed tray seemed to burst into life and were trying to burst through the fabric.

Mr Lawrence moved round the bench. He aimed a long jet of water down my spine before returning the container to the work top. He ran one hand slowly over the bumps of my back and cupped my bottom. With the fingers of his other hand, he rubbed the tips of my nipples in a circular motion that made the breath catch in my throat and warm dribbles began to run down my legs. The earth on his fingers stained the dress in two perfect circles around my breasts. He moved his fingers over my swollen lips and, one by one, I took them into my mouth. His fingers were sticky with fresh earth and I can't imagine what I was doing sucking them.

I had forgotten to put on any knickers and his other hand was stroking the tense bare flesh of my bottom. His fingers slipped into the sticky pool between my legs and I often wonder what may have happened next, the next as it happens being the door bursting open and Mother standing there with the light behind her like the monster that woke me from my dreams.

'Lucy. Lucy. You. You...'

She crossed the shed in one long stride and hit Mr Lawrence across the face with such a hard slap it left four white stripes on his cheek.

'You animal. You oaf. Get out this minute.'

Jake must have wondered what all the fuss was about and stood there with his pink tongue lolling from his mouth. Mr Lawrence stroked the dog's head. He stared boldly back at Mother and the look they exchanged said more about their relationship than I ever could have imagined and I would think about that later in the day.

Mother turned to me. 'What would your father say? What would Mr Daviditz say?'

After the momentary shock of Mother's appearance I did the only thing I could do. I ran back through the garden and into the house crying and didn't stop until Mother became bored and said she didn't care what I did or who I did it with as long as we kept it from Mr Daviditz because he was a solicitor and a Christian and a man who wouldn't tolerate that sort of thing.

'Lucy, you have to know, you're very...Mediterranean,' she said, as if the word had the taste of a stale olive. 'You're the type.'

'The type?'

'The type men are going to interfere with.'

'You think so?'

'Look, I really can't deal with you as well as everything else,' she said. 'Don't you understand, your father lost everything. There's no money, no finishing school, no future. Nothing.'

I turned and looked into her eyes. 'Everything's going to be all right,' I told her.

'The worst thing I ever did was allow you to go to school in Italy. You're like a child.'

'I'm doing my best,' I said.

'That's not what I mean, Lucy, and you know it.'

She bit her think lips as if holding back everything else she wanted to say.

We became quiet and watched Sylvester through the French windows. Simon Daviditz was coming for lunch and I was thinking about what I was going to wear.

I kissed Mother on the cheek, something I rarely did, and bounded three at a time up the stairs.

I put on the first CD I laid my hands on and sang along to the music as I peered into the wardrobe. One thing I had learned from Nonna is that a woman should always dress for the occasion. I opened the drawers and went through my blouses and tee-shirts, tight jeans, hipsters, cargo pants, flares, little halters, long pants, hot pants, it's all so very difficult. I took off my clothes and studied myself in the long mirror.

My breasts were round and full and stayed propped up by themselves. They were lovely and I really couldn't resist touching them. My hips and bottom were small like a boy's and my thighs that still tingled didn't quite touch when I stood straight. Daddy was an Italian and, like him, I have brown eyes, honey-colored skin and thick dark hair I'd always worn in pigtails, even when I knew it had become old fashioned for a girl of my age. Just as my breasts had started filling out, so silken threads as fine as angel hair had formed in a triangle that was now dense and soft, a little nest below my bikini line.

I'd read in one of Mother's magazines that for a woman less is always more and so a bikini must be perfect. I had a yellow one with red flowers that was a size too small and when I put it on I looked like a girl who didn't know she had grown up and looked more girlish from not knowing it. I turned to look at my rear. My shoulder blades stuck out and my bottom that I'd thought belonged to a boy had grown perfectly round and now belonged to me. I had wanted to be a boy for as long as I could remember but sensed there was a lot more to being a girl. I ran the tips of my fingers over my pink nipples and they prickled as if from pins and needles. I turned for a sideways look and really had to blink several times and look again. Mr Lawrence had tricked my breasts into growing a whole half size bigger since he'd tried to plant me in one of his pots.

I took my hair out of pigtails and combed it over my shoulders, turning the ends under. I studied the new style, then changed it back again. Daddy had once told me that although I was growing up I shouldn't be in too much of a hurry. Latin men understood these things and I suppose it was the Latin in me that had awoken that morning.

My gold crucifix was hanging over the side of the dressing table. I put it on, squirted perfume in the air and stood in the shower as it rained over me. I was about to leave the bedroom when I heard Mother opening the door downstairs.

Mr Daviditz had arrived.

I waited until he was in the drawing room, crept down the stairs and out through the kitchen to the garden. I had my iPod, a towel and a bottle of sun oil which I set down on the lawn where the apple tree obscures the view from the French windows.

'Lucy, Simon's here,' I heard Mother call in her sugary voice and I rushed off like an eager puppy to greet him.

'Ah, Lucy, Lucy as juicy as ever,' he said.

He thought this was awfully clever and had said it before. He didn't notice Mother biting her lips.

I was breathless from all my running about and, as he lowered his glasses, his eyes fell piously to the gold cross throbbing in the dark hollow between my breasts.

Mother's expression made it clear that she intended telling me to go and put on something more fitting, but was so relieved by my warm display she decided to let it drop. Mr Daviditz was dressed in white trousers and a dark green polo shirt that welled in a soft balloon over a woven brown leather belt. He had lots of fine pale hair of which he was clearly very proud, red cheeks, damp hands and a wispy moustache that he fiddled with incessantly. He was carrying a bouquet for Mother and broke off one of the blooms for me. I put it between my teeth and skipped off back to the garden.

Sylvester bolted up the tree and sat there sharpening his paws on the bark. I covered my front with oil and plugged the iPod into my ears. I tried to calculate how long it would take before Mr Daviditz came but grew tired of the game and just listened to the music. I had made a point of being unkind to Simon Daviditz since that day at the funeral when he couldn't keep his eyes off me, but according to Mother abrupt mood swings in teenagers are the result of hormones and are perfectly normal.

My skin was just beginning to get that tight feeling that comes when you stay too long in the sun when a shadow brought a welcome relief. Mr Daviditz carried a drink complete with a straw and ice cubes that tinkled against the glass.

'A spritzer,' he said like a conspirator.

He knelt down beside me as I drank: fizzy water with white wine and quite disgusting. I sucked on the straw.

'Delicious,' I said.

'Yes,' he paused. 'Yes, indeed.'

'I can't reach my back, would you?' I gave him the sun oil and his hands were shaking as he took the bottle.

I turned over and loosened my top. He spread the oil over my shoulders, his cautious hands moving slowly down my arms, around my waist, one leg, then the other. He pulled each one of my toes, then moved with greater confidence back up my legs. He began massaging the base of my spine, each downward motion peeling back my bikini bottom as if he were paring a ripe apple just fallen from the tree. As if by friction, with each movement I eased the weight from my hips.

For some reason I had started thinking about Mr Lawrence and it only occurred to me now that he had the same eyes as Daddy, the same as me.

'That feels lovely,' I said. 'You have such soft hands you should have been a doctor.'

'I did consider of it. Then the law got me.'

I gave an encouraging laugh. 'What a pity, you could have examined me all over when I was ill,' I told him.

He was gasping like an old train as he carried on working his palms up and down, up and down, and before I died of boredom I activated his secret plan by eliminating the pull of gravity. I raised my hips clean from the ground and with one more tug at the elastic, Mr Daviditz had my bikini briefs down around my knees. I lowered myself to the towel and wriggled like a freshly caught fish.

He dribbled oil over the small my back and began fondling the two moons of my bottom, his fingers edging into the crease. I waited for that moist feeling to come but it didn't happen this time and I imagined Mr Daviditz didn't have the touch. He finally spread my cheeks with trembling fingers and we remained motionless as if time were suspended.

'Lunch,' I heard Mother sing out from the kitchen, and I couldn't help laughing as Mr Daviditz fell backwards and hit his head against the tree. Sylvester leapt down from the branch from where he'd been watching, hissed and ran off.

'Deary, deary me, look what's happened.'

Mr Daviditz jerked the red-flowered briefs back in place before lurching to his feet. I turned over, reaching for my top, and was unable to conceal my breasts. I looked coyly up into his eyes. Mr Daviditz seemed so intense it was as if we'd just been to another funeral and I thought old people took things which were only a bit of fun far too seriously.

'Come on,' he said. I took the hand he offered and he studied my face as if written in my flushed cheeks were clues to his destiny.

'Thank you,' I whispered before he could say anything and it occurred to me that, not one, but two men had interfered with me that day and if I'd kept a diary it would have given me something to write about.

Mother watched us making our way back across the lawn. There was a look in her eyes, the same look she had given Mr Lawrence when she slapped his face, but now that look was for me.

'Lucy, you're not a child. Do get dressed,' she said.

I did, demurely, in a white skirt and blouse.

Mr Daviditz at lunch was very attentive to both Mother and his moustache and, while he practically ignored me, I sat there studying Mother's vile collection of teapots arranged on the shelves. I skipped pudding and wandered through the rooms looking at paintings and ornaments, the family snaps in silver frames, the polished beams on the low ceiling.

I loved Ickham Manor and I suppose it was hardly surprising. It was my house, my very own, left to me in a trust, and now that Daddy was dead I wanted everything to remain the same as it always was. I sat at the piano but my mind just couldn't focus on Mozart and I gave up trying. I settled in the alcove at the end of the drawing room and flicked through an old picture book with a girl and a pony on the cover.

The story was about poor little Lizzie Dripping who wanted to ride her pony at the gymkhana, but the pony had a tummy upset *just like people*. Lizzie had washy blue eyes, a yellow pony tail poking out of her riding hat and was so exceedingly dull all she could do was sit and cry until the pony felt so irritated by her it got better. Lizzie went to the gymkhana and won a pink ribbon. I had read the book a hundred of times when I was little, but now it made me want to go to the bathroom and yuck up the spritzer.

I scrolled down to the new Dallas McTee on the iPod and was just about to stretch out on the floor when Mother and Mr Daviditz came waltzing in looking awfully pleased with themselves.

They sat together on the sofa. Mother is an English blonde with the blue grey eyes of the Atlantic and was wearing the same intense look as Lizzie Dripping.

'We've got something to tell you,' she said.

Mr Daviditz's cheeks were redder than ever as he took her hand. 'I've asked Hester, your mother, to be my wife,' he announced.

There was a long silence while we all waited for someone to speak. I noticed the nerve in Mother's neck throb with a moment's impatience.

'Are you happy?' she finally asked.

I studied them both and wondered if they were going to have children

'Oh, yes,' I said. 'Very.'

Mr Daviditz looked relieved. 'Now, we should do something to celebrate. What would you like to do?'

I took a big breath, put my finger to my lips, and gazed about the room.

'Anything you like,' he added.

I was still thinking.

'Come along, Lucy,' said Mother.

'I know,' I replied. 'Let's go into Canterbury and buy some new underwear.'

Reviews for The Secret Life of Girls

"Bella loves sex. Boys, girls, a young nun, an older man or two. She's a girl who can't say no to her restless desires and longings. Sex for Bella is fun "people take it much too seriously.

"Then, she discovers her conniving and voyeuristic stepfather has stolen her house from under her nose and now sex becomes her weapon of revenge. Without sex, this would have been a pretty good coming of age novel. With Chloe's fine eye for the erotic, it's a little gem I can't recommend enough.

"A passing thought, you also get the feeling reading these pages that, more than the other novels from this fine writer, The Secret Life of Girls is more than a touch autobiographical."
LARRY ROLAND TAYLOR, AMAZON.COM

"Simply put, this is the best book of erotica I have ever read."
D. LUCIUS RHINEHART, AMAZON.COM

"Bella is a very naughty and very horny girl. She lets her family's 40 year old gardener rub her nipples and finger her pussy. At her elite finishing school, she enjoys it when a nun licks her pussy in the catacombs. Now that Bella knows how wonderful sex is, she enthusiastically deflowers the other girls in her dorm. But when her wicked stepfather brutally spanks her and forces his cock down her throat, she gets her revenge by entrapping him in a lewd act on video. Soon, Bella is living the fast life as a singer and porn star. It thrills her when men spank her adorable ass. The mix of pain and pleasure is intoxicating. Her attitude is aptly summed up by one of her favorite songs: I'm a Bitch and I Know It."

QSM – QUALITY SM

The fourth extract is an orgy scene that comes about three-quarters of the way through *The Gift of Girls,* published by Nexus in 2009. In this novel, Magdalena is about to start university majoring in mathematics. She is tricked into becoming a sex slave to a group of wealthy powerful men and can't make up her mind whether she loves or hates the experience.

NOTE:

One critic of EL James has written that she 'must have swallowed a thesaurus', and another accuses her of making references to classic literature. Readers, as well as writers, should be aware that erotica is a literary genre with the flexibility to embrace every facet of the language. Furthermore, the style and feel of the language will depend on the main character. Anastasia Steels is a literature student, of course she has read Jane Austin and Emily Brontë, dipped into Freud and enjoys Christian introducing her to Delibes's *The Flower Duet* from the opera *Lakmé*.

Back-cover blurb:

Magdalena Wallace is good at math and scores a great summer job as an intern at city accountants Roche-Marshall where she is trusted to check accounts. She doesn't tell her boss, the darkly mysterious Simon Roche, that she works nights as a waitress at Rebels Casino dressed in fishnets and a corset. Magdalena is desperate. She needs the money.

When Magdalena learns a 'secret' system from a high-roller, she plays the tables and loses her university savings. She then dips into clients' money and loses that as well. What's more, Simon Roche has found out. Should he go to the police and report Magdalena, or will she agree to be his slave until the debt is paid? She

*agrees but never envisaged just how far she will have
to go to break even.*

Being & Fantasy

Every man is different. They are like snowflakes. They have
their patterns and designs, their character and temperaments,
flavor and tempo, their fantasies and fervent thirsts. They are
as boys with toys that have moveable parts.

Some are big, so meaty and solid you feel in your belly
the pulse of their burning balls of fire. Others are petite,
slender as lolly sticks, and it needs all the cunning vibrations
of your thigh muscles and vagina walls to remunerate their
feverish efforts.

Some are in a rush. Wham Bam Thank You Ma'am. In
and out as if there's a fire on the first floor; or the last virgin is
about to be sacrificed. They impale you like spear fishermen
on the South China Seas, like javelin throwers at the
Olympics, like dart players in the pub, leaving their marker in
you or over you.

I'm in there.

I'm outta here.

You're just the quickie before more urgent things drive
them onwards and upwards. They scurry and their sweat. They
lose their hair. Their focus. They know there's a secret. They
feel it. Sense it. They calculate if they move fast enough
they'll get there, they'll win the race, they'll learn the secret.

But they never will. Those men are the progeny of the
legendary hare. It is the tortoise who wins the race. Unhurried,
dogged, deliberate, the tortoise knows that life is a mystery
solved with persistence. He's prehistoric. He has been among
us for a million years, and when you sift through every grain
of earthly promise, the seed that flowers into the brightest
bloom is the slow-growing, seldom seen erotic. The tortoise
knows that.

The hares are narcissists, the alpha males, the ego-maniacs terrified that just around the corner there may be a better hole to bore, a new bit of stuff that's sexier, prettier, curvier, younger, more flexible, more intelligent, with longer legs, a longer tongue, bigger tits, a better ass, a better attitude. These guys are in such a hurry they have never found the time to learn that of all life's pleasures the erotic is at the peak, above the tree line and clouds, that what they give out will come back a hundred fold. A thousand fold. What a sad Neanderthal bunch of braindeads they are. They've never grown up from being schoolboys. They are and will remain forever on the bottom field.

Other men are patient, ponderous, a philatelist with a rare stamp, or a scientist with a new species of flora. Like a mathematician with algebraic puzzles, or a topographer surveying land, they want to analyze every angle and turn, every hill and dale, every curve and fissure with its moist secrets and inexplicable erogenous zones where a mere touch or a breath can set pulses racing and knees atremble. These connoisseurs of the female form want to smack you, spank you, whip and cane your white flesh until it is patterned with the geometry of their deepest lusts. Your body is an abacus and the maestro sets your beads flying.

Why does a man want to beat you?

He wants to beat you because in the thrall of domination and submission you find the chemistry of sexual oblivion. You find your true self. You find the absolute: total sexual gratification. Weird, I know, but true and I would advise every girl to try it.

To the stamp collector you are the celebrated Penny Black. He wants you in his album below a sheet of tissue, in a display case, nakedly on show. He wants you this way and that: prone as a missionary spouse doing her duty to king maker and country; looming above like a harem concubine who reminds him oddly of mummy in those days when she peered down at baby in his cot and the love in her eyes stirred the little member sleeping in his diaper. He wants to see you on the floor balanced on hands and toes, breasts swinging like pendulums striking the hour in a grandfather clock, back at an angle, the pink feast of your pussy open like a rip in the universe, soft as velvet, sweet as rose petals below the dark gaze of your puckered anus.

Agh, the angst of choice: the dripping, sweet smelling rose or the pungent fruit from the Judas tree?

Or both!

Like the tortoise.

I felt detached, freed from the chains of choice, my nerve endings keened with a desire for esoteric wisdom, for pleasures and experiences on the very edge of my imagination. I wanted to swim like a fish and fly like a bird. When you are young and naked with your life before you, anything might happen. Every girl fantasizes about having a stream of lovers. I was living the fantasy. It was hallucinogenic, a drug trip on nothing more than a flute of champagne and a feast of fresh semen. My brain was humming, my body was bathed in perspiration. I was the perfect object, the guava hanging ripe and shiny from the Tree in the Garden of Eden ready to be used, abused, defiled and worshipped. I was the virgin sacrifice.

With my wrists fastened to the bed and stretched above me, I could smell the almond scent of my underarms. My heart was beating fast, my stomach muscles clenching and unclenching. Being bound was a dance of conflicting emotions: arousal and acquiescence, and panic, too, like the moment before the curtain rises and you go on stage.

After Sergio Buenavista left me with the aftershocks of that bell-ringing finale, the first man to come through the door immediately unclasped the bracelets from the rings set on the side of the bed and set me on all fours. My well-tanned backside like a monkey's mating display was waggling in the air, my back bowed in a shallow curve, my breasts swayed and my nipples were pinging like fireworks.

Men like this position, this simian pose, down on hands and knees, my spread cheeks like open curtains revealing the treasure kept hidden within the neat nips and tucks of my pretty bum which I could see in all its shiny glory in the clever arrangement of the mirrors. The man said something in a language that made no sense to me, spat on his fingers, wet the mine shaft of my back passage and shoved his cock straight in that innocent chasm. His trousers were about his ankles, his jacket slapped about like the sail of a ship and no sooner had he started than he stopped.

'Turn, turn about,' he said urgently.

I turned, dropped down on my haunches, took his thrusting dagger in my mouth, massaged his balls, and in two seconds he was pumping warm sperm down my throat, a stream of 100% protein. He took the back of my head in his two hands, pushed in harder, his blunt helmet tickled my tonsils, and I could taste the sweet girlie secretion of my own bottom, and not bad at all.

He withdrew his withering apparatus and withdrew himself from the room without a word, and I wasn't surprised when I was later told that he was the Prime Minister from one of those anonymous countries that used to be a part of the old Soviet bloc and which would have remained forgotten if it weren't for their oil and gas, for the pipeline snaking its way underground to the new container ports built by the Americans on the Caspian Sea.

How judicious the men of the New World Order, I thought, to draw these old communist apparatchiks into their complex game, this bacchanal of free market sex and global domination. And how fascinating that the delights of the flesh and the demands of commerce should be so manifestly intertwined, two lovers carved from the same block of stone.

It was an obvious market strategy, but not one that had occurred to me studying economics at Saint Sebastian. I had lived as most people live like a horse in blinders and felt as if the scales had peeled from my eyes. There is so much to this life that the man in the street doesn't understand and I felt honored to have this glimpse of the secret. Like Milly, I could see suddenly that being a part of this world above the clouds was a privilege as well as a pleasure.

I sighed with contentment and wriggled like a fish. The room was warm. The round bed was huge, a pearl white dais, and I lay there like a precious stone in the jewelers, my image passing endlessly from mirror to mirror and as I gazed at my dissociated form my only regret was that there was no time for reflection among all those reflections. The door closed and the door opened. It was like a pub door, a revolving door that led to the tower room and another man I didn't recall was making his way in.

He was plump around the middle and wore a clip-on bow tie – *déclassé* mother would have said; *nouveau riche*. He unceremoniously unclipped his tie and pulled open his shirt to reveal the lush coat of fur covering his chest. He tugged his black leather belt from the loops of his trousers with a saucy snap and doubled the length into his right hand.

'I'm Kurt. You want to play around?' he said; it sounded like a line from a Quentin Tarantino movie.

'Ooo, yes please,' I replied.

He was standing between the door and the bed. He approached, slapping his palm with the leather belt. I rolled backwards from my prone position and landed on my feet. He chased me around the perimeter of the bed, wielding the belt like a horse whip, but I was far too fast for him. The lash cracked the air behind me but the tongue never reached my wiggling bottom. He tried a new tactic and ran across the bed. I allowed him to get close and did a back flip, landing on my feet. His eyes came out on stalks and, as he continued the chase, I did front rolls round and round the circular room, Kurt whooping and shouting and splitting the air with the bite of his belt.

He was tired a long time before me. He made one last desperate charge, tripped over his shiny shoes and collapsed, crumpling like road kill against the mirror. He sat up and watched, shaking his head in disbelief as I coolly stretched backwards, placed my hands on the floor behind me so that my feet were facing one way and my hands the other. I arched my body in a perfect circle, making the sign of Ω, the 24th and last letter of the Greek alphabet, I do recall; in astronomy Omega refers to the density of the universe, as Pi is a mathematical constant which represents the ratio of a circle's circumference to its diameter.

God, would I ever leave school behind me?

Where was I?

Agh, yes, I walked very slowly towards him like some imaginary creature from the Island of Doctor Moreau, my hair a long mane dragging behind me, my open pussy like the eye of the Cyclops.

Kurt stood to admire this arrangement of enticement and suppleness. He dropped his belt, flipped his erection from his trousers and cautiously slipped it inside me. In this position I could do nothing but maintain my balance and use all my powers of pussy control to clasp the length of his cock, my vaginal muscles clenching and releasing with contractions.

I got the feeling that this guy was one of those speed jockeys, the wham bam off to the races type. But with my slippery young crack presented in this unique way, he became a tortoise; he discovered his serene self. He took his time, filled me to the brim with his pudgy thick cock, withdrew and pushed in again, slowly, slowly, until I felt the spasm gripping his body focus like a laser beam around the head of his engulfed penis. He paused, as do the old on the stairs, or parachutists making their first jump, then released his sperm, pumping the stuff out in slow steady jerks as if wringing the last drop of water from a canteen in the middle of the desert. He was panting like an old cart horse.

'Very gut. Very gut. You very gut,' he moaned.

He slid from me and, pushing from my fingers, I straightened up in one effortless motion. He was spent, but I was relaxed, refreshed, re-energized. Sperm was oozing from me, creaming my thighs, coating my crotch with the aroma of lust, that mesmerising scent, that supernatural elixir that persuaded the Greeks to launch a thousand ships – it wasn't Helen's face that drove them to folly and war. How absurd. It was her allure, her looks, her mystery, her magic and, most of all, her smell. The Greeks understood the powers of Omega and Pi but not the whims of a woman.

I breathed in deeply through my nose. I could smell all about me the reek of lasciviousness, the matted copse of my glistening pubes sheltering the lips of my sodden pussy, that clump of fur I loved to stroke and fondle like a little pet or a stuffed toy.

I felt in my round room of many mirrors like a satiated little animal, like a red-assed monkey in the midst of a marvellous experiment, like a bird in a mirrored cage. I was the cocoon girl metamorphosed into the butterfly woman, ensnared by Simon Roche, yet free to be all that I am and all that I may ever be. I may with my nudity and bondage straps have lost facets of my individuality, the memory of who I thought I was, but the men who shed their seed in the dome of my vagina lost aspects of their individuality, too, that only through merging your self into the oneness of pure debauchery could you reach the heights of the erotic.

I realised, too, that I had been thinking along these libidinous lines for a long time. It wasn't sudden. Not really. Didn't I, in my quest to learn how to beat the casinos, allow Sandy Cunningham to take me on a totally licentious journey? I had told myself immediately before and immediately after that it was awful, shameful, a terrible trial but, if truth be told, it came as easily as breathing. My clothes were off and his cock was up my bum on that hotel bed in about the same amount of time that it takes for me to swim two lengths of the swimming pool.

That was me. The real me. That was the girl who had begun to appear in the mirror during my last year at Saint Sebastian, the look in her eyes growing ever more knowing, more aware, more sensual. The girl in the reflection was replacing the inexperienced schoolgirl gazing into the long mirror in the shower room and, as her body changed, swelled, reformed, the girl I had been slowly vanished to be reborn as the girl I am.

A grin widened across my lips as I recalled that day after Sister Benedict caned me and I shed an ocean of pee over the stone flags of her office floor. I had been ashamed, of course, but the exhibitionist in me was animated by this bizarre turn of events. Until the day I die, I will never forget the look of shock and awe on the sister's wizened little face as that stream like a burst water main kept hissing out, rich smelling and steamy, a golden lake that swallowed her little black shoes.

As I lay back on that round bed in that circular room aromatic with lust, it was obvious that I should have found my way into the New World. As people are born to be leaders, to win Olympic medals, or clean lavatories, I suppose, we are each one of us born with a purpose, a talent. We speak of talent as a gift. The secret of life is to discover who you are, to be the best you can be, to nurture your gift and share your gift as an artist shares the gift of his written or carved or painted work. When we are moved by an object of art, we are grateful that the writer or artist created that work, that he dug deep in the quarries of his gift and brought it to the surface.

The girls gathered at Black Spires were conscious of their gift. They found genuine pleasure in sharing their gift, and it occurred to me that unhappiness, depression and disappointment awaited those unable to explore and enjoy the miracle of their divine talent, that one special gift.

The girls were slender, ethereal, dainty, svelte, yet with perfectly round bottoms, lean waists and unusually full breasts. Even barefoot, they walked as if in heels, their naturally full hair heavy on well-defined shoulders, their eyes gleaming like stars in the sky. Naked, their bodies ingeniously cut by the six leather bands, they were a breed apart, a different species, and it was a relief and a strange joy to know that I was one of them. I had fooled myself into thinking I was born for a career calculating numbers, although I had, I recalled, begun to suspect as my bottom curved and my breasts filled out that my gift lie elsewhere, less in figures than my figure. Sister Benedict had known it, too. That bottom, her eyes informed me, had to be spanked.

Girls like Melissa and Sarah were not born for this life, as they were not born to taste the Sister's cruel cane. Melissa carried too much avoirdupois, big thighs, breasts like udders, objects of amusement more than desire. Sarah was anorexic with sunken cheeks and arms thin as matchsticks. Girls required slenderness, not thinness, a sense of grace without heaviness. Girls born with the gift were born blessed with the eternal, perfectly-proportioned physique of the feminine ideal: the beauty that must be profaned at the height of the erotic in order to reach the erotic, the core of the gift that sleeps deep within and awakes in the chosen woman.

If we look at engravings of Helen of Troy on ancient coins and shields, or the maidens copulating with men and gods carved on the walls of caves in India, or at the girls offering up their bottoms to be thrashed and filmed on fareastmedia.com, through three millennia they all have the same willowy ripe busty innocence, they all have that ill-defined flawlessness men want to beat and adore.

There is a moment, a precise second, when a girl becomes a woman. It's that moment when you notice men looking at you and you know what they are looking for. They are measuring your breasts pushing through your high-buttoned blouse, the roundness of that saucy bottom wiggling by in a pleated skirt down the high street, the turn of your plump lips they want to consume, as the Duc de Peralada had done as soon as he got the chance. It's the time when Sister Benedict starts bending you over the desk so that she can lower your knickers and tan your backside, beat all that ripe sensuality out of her convent.

Whatever it was Mother Superior hoped to achieve, beyond her own gratification, it didn't work. It never works. Girls like me have to be what they were born to be. There is in us all the propensity for all extremes both good and evil, the escape valve that saves us from mediocrity. Are we that different from the kidnapper, the assassin, the thief? If temptation is put in your way, as it was put in mine, is it not natural to take the prize, slip the gold ring on your finger, the $100 bill into your palm, to transfer £3,100 from the company account into your own? If you were a fat cat banker with the prerogative to pay yourself a million dollar bonus would you be able to resist?

The men who came into that room were tempted and lured by this eager young girl bonded to the New World Order, bonded by black bracelets and anklets, with breasts yearning to be touched and a lush smelling crotch that grew wetter and more desirable with each coupling. Those men were doing what comes naturally to powerful men, to all men, I imagine, and it was both a surprise and a revelation to realize that it came naturally to me, too.

I felt no shame, no ignominy, no doubts. Heaven forbid! I felt good about myself. It was a pleasure parading around starkers. It was pure bliss being crowned the queen of the mirror room and taking those men whose names I didn't even know into my body without the bourgeois, time-wasting game of getting to know you, without preliminaries and foreplay. I was a spring flower bursting with nectar and they were a swarm of hornets darting into my sticky parts with the gift of their juicy liquids. I was created, it seems, to spend time on my back, on my front, on my knees like a red-assed monkey. I was born to enjoy sex in every possible form and position, and what better time to indulge this craving than now, at the age of eighteen, at my succulent best.

My life could have been so different, the good 'A' levels blowing me like a feather on the wind into a career in an accountancy firm in the City. That may have been predicted by the stars, by the geometric hexagrams of the *I Ching*, but I'd experienced a premonition the moment I tightened the corset on the hostess costume at Rebels that there were other potentials in me ripe for exploration. I still might return to my studies, I thought, become a business woman, an entrepreneur. And, if I did, I would always, I'm sure, be thankful to have had this experience at Black Spires, this chance to delve into the very deepest parts of my primordial nature.

I stretched and sighed with a sense of well-being, a feeling I hadn't really had since daddy announced that he was selling the house in the country, our flat in Lowndes Square, the Andy Warhol print of Clint Eastward he'd acquired in a moment's excitement in New York; his cherished Cessna SkyCatcher; mummy's jewelry, by brother's future, my own. I had cried for a week. Mummy was still crying. Then I woke up. I dried my eyes, I applied to be an accountancy intern and I took Melissa's advice, and dressed to kill for that interview with fate. The path through life, it seems, is like a helter-skelter and once you push off from the top of the chute you spiral round and round and down and down until with your head spinning you arrive at who you are.

We are, each of us, the master of our own ship. I felt positive, optimistic, more alive. Something had crossed over in me, perhaps it was the reality of growing up. When I strode naked through the Roche-Marshall building, it wasn't only my clothes that I'd left behind. I had left the child, the schoolgirl, the past, the fear. I would have to redirect my destiny, make my own future, and it started here, now, in this round room of many mirrors among the most powerful men in the world.

I had quite forgotten Kurt, the Quentin Tarantino extra. I lay there on the big bed enjoying my own smell, as all animals do, and watched as he pushed his belt back through the loops in his trousers.

'Very gut,' he said.

Then he was gone and another man appeared. The fourth, was it? Maybe the seventh? Perhaps the tenth? Was it an odd number or even? A prime or square root? It was hard to keep score, to keep count. And it occurred to me that under normal circumstances a girl might sleep with eight or ten men in a month, even a year. In that old Norman mansion in the aura of orgy, there need be no end to the number of men you could drain and entertain in one long night. I lay, spread like a star fish on that circular ten foot platform staring at an infinity of Magdalenas in the mirror tiles of the dome above my head, each reflection a different angle, a different aspect, a different suggestion of what we might be in life.

The door opened. I watched the man who I had first seen spanking the twins, before doing them as a pair, approach with another, quite similar-looking man in the same sort of dinner suit, the same swagger and look of confidence.

'The oyster in the shell,' said the first man, gazing at me spread out on the bed.

The other was removing his clothes. They both did. Beads of sweat were coursing between my breasts; there must have been underfloor heating and the temperature was rising.

The Fifty Shades of Grey Phenomena

Ravisher One licked away the sweat, tasting me, and started nibbling my nipples, his stiffening cock pushing gently against my hipbone. Number Two spread my legs and pushed his tongue into that discreet arch containing the firebird, that mythical creature men know is there even if they can't always find it. He found it.

This was nice, one above and one below, my body a playground for inquisitive teeth and tongues.

'Wow, she's wet,' said Number Two, an American.

'It's my hormones,' I whispered and he laughed.

Number One straddled my neck and tapped my closed lips with his mauve helmet, knock, knock, knock, and I opened the door, allowed it entrance, this salty, fishy thing that had been locked in his underpants with a vague hint of the emerald twins, and I wondered if the two girls had the same smell, or if all girls were different, that like fingerprints we are blessed with an individual scent. It was something I thought I might study when I got the chance.

Number One's silky cock slithered down my throat and I did my trick as it drew back again. I stippled the tip of my tongue around the indentation. Then, I pressed down with my teeth before opening my gullet once more and drawing it down, down, deep inside the sense cathedral of my gaping mouth.

Number Two had given up invigorating my clitoris. Sitting with legs spread for balance, he lifted my thighs over his torso and his cock went scurrying like a hungry serpent up inside my insatiable pussy.

They were like two men rowing a boat, getting into a steady rhythm, two cocks gliding inside me at the same time, one in my mouth, the other in my vagina, and I knew before the night was through I would know what it was to take a third, to be filled with cock, and honestly couldn't wait.

It was deep-rooted in me to want to overstep the limits, to sell my soul in the surreal frenzy of orgy. Mummy believed a woman's role was to be obedient, something she taught me but never practised herself. It made me sad that my beautiful mother had never learned that discipline and corporal punishment weren't humiliating and undignified. *Au contraire*. All flesh pleasures are empowering, emancipating. Those black leather bands decorating my naked body were a symbol of freedom, a sign that I had broken the chains of an imposed and artificial respectability, a morality that belonged to that part of society that was deadly dull and really not for me.

A woman is fulfilled by being filled. We are born with wet vacant places designed to be plugged. This is a truth, an axiom, and understanding that is at the heart of female liberation. We are taught to be ambitious, to shatter the glass ceiling, but this I thought was bogus and wrong. Our role as animals is to continue the species. Our role as women is to seek the quintessence and core of our sexuality. Knowing that, feeling it on my skin, was like opening a safe door and finding the key of life.

As the man with the cock in my mouth stiffened, the spasm clanged the bell on my vibrating tonsils and the echo travelled through my gut, into my belly, ricocheting over the walls of my vagina and gripping the cock delving down inside me. As the first released a gout of semen, the second answered like it was a tennis ball to beat back over the net. He tensed, he paused, and let go his load. They were shivering and trembling, but I felt relaxed, fed, nurtured, in control of my gift.

They rolled away, panting for breath, and a third man appeared through the revolving door. He threw off his clothes as he dissected the room, dived in among the sweating bodies and began kissing me violently, grabbing my hipbones, squeezing my breasts until they tingled with pain, biting down into that part of my neck just above the collar bone that sends tremors of pleasure shimmying down your backbone. He was grunting and panting like a wild dog with fresh prey. I wriggled from his grasp and, as I was about to vault from the bed, Number One caught me in a rugger tackle and swung me over on to my stomach.

On seeing my red bum, the new arrival buried his head between my cheeks and drilled his long tongue deep into the hidden valley. He came out panting.

'Delicious,' he yelled.

His cock soon followed, jabbing into me, a young boxer in the ring leading with a series of swift rights. His arms coiled under me, filling his palms with my breasts. He took my nipples in the thumbs and first fingers of both hands and squeezed down so hard I squealed in ecstasy, in that peculiar pain sensation that isn't pain in any normal sense.

In one swift movement, he rolled on to his back, and kept pushing into my tight bum with me spread-eagled across his broad chest. Number One, who had just climaxed in my mouth, had found enough vigor to join the fray and climbed on top, pushing his cock limply up into the pool of semen left by Number Two. Number Two straddled me and the guy below me in order to push his pussy-juiced member into my gaping mouth.

Your wish is my command. Ask and it shall be given. Knock and the door shall be opened.

It seemed as if the moment I imagined taking three men at once, the universe answered my call and I lay there, as lucky as any girl can be, our quartet like the jazz musicians in the grand hall finding harmony and rhythm, our bodies joined like a machine mining precious substances.

I could see fully now the benefit of the many mirrors. I was facing the ceiling, my mouth filled with cock, but I could see in a long series of reflections a fourth man enter the room with Milly. They were holding hands like lovers. When they reached the bed, the man stepped from his clothes and lay down on his back. Milly straddled him, took his cock up inside her, and the alpha male with his cock in my mouth removed his member and transferred it to Milly's mouth.

What did I taste like, I wondered?

We were four men and two girls.

A sextet.

I smiled as I stretched my aching jaw. I am an instrument in a sextet, a high note in the New World Order. It occurred to me that these men of big business spilling their seed together were united in a way that a thousand board meetings could never achieve. They needed no contracts, no handshake. Their naked body was their bond, their signature, and I and Milly and all the girls at Black Spires were the links in the chain that held them together. The glue, the gum, the gluck. They needed us. We were a part of something bigger and more important than I was able to understand, perhaps more important than I could understand.

This, I thought, is what life is. This is how it works. People want to let go, strip naked and follow their base instincts wherever they may lead them. The masters of the universe understood this: when you have everything, wealth, power, respect, achievement, connections, what remains?

The orgy.

All the people out there reading their newspapers and watching their TV sets were listening to politicians and pundits with about as much power to intervene in events as the captain of the *Titanic* as his ship struck that fateful iceberg. Everything that Milly had said earlier made sense now on that round bed with our stripped bodies magnified to infinity.

The man below me shot a cannonball of hot spunk up my bum and a little squirt small as a tear was released by the man in my vagina. He'd done well. I'd done well. Our bodies collapsed in a boisterous pile. There were lips and mouths everywhere, kissing, licking, biting, and I'm sure I saw Number Four, the man who'd arrived with Milly, take Number three's cock in his mouth, and I thought, why not, they are probably partners. I found myself kissing Milly and realised that kissing men would never have quite the same appeal. Girls' lips are soft, tender, sugary, plump and taste of heaven. They are made to be kissed and being kissed was a pleasure every bit as great as having three cocks filling my three orifices.

As our lips parted and another cock wound it way into my mouth, it was impossible to know who it belonged to and this lack of a face and name, of the man's persona, his character, his being, made it all the more pleasurable. There was an equality on that circular dais, that lozenge of white linen. Our individualities were consumed in the pure sweet decadence of the orgy, an almost spiritual ritual that allowed my soul to grow wings and fly.

Others were appearing in one and twos, the emerald twins like Siamese twins, the links of their bracelets and anklets joined left to right so that they walked in step, swinging their arms like soldiers. The girl with the panorama of tattoos led the older man with snowy hair by his small erection. He looked dazed and boyish. I watched another girl I hadn't seen before appear on all fours, the rings on her choker linked to the belt of a Cabinet Minister recently resigned 'to spend more time with his family.'

Now I knew what the euphemism meant. This was his family. We were his family. In the photographs of him in the newspapers he had looked tense and anguished. In the mirror room he was naked, relaxed, content, the belt like a dog lead in one hand, his free hand nursing his erection. He paused and shot a stream of spunk over the girl's back. She had reached the edge of the bed and another man immediately shoved his cock in her pretty mouth.

The tattooed girl had reached the side of the bed at the same time. She was shuffling the wrinkled flesh of the older man in one hand and in her free hand another man had found his way into her palm, her arms moving like the beams on an ancient spinning jenny, up and down, up and down. The Maasai was performing a belly dance about the Arab sheik, the bells about her ankles ringing, her spiralling hands finding their way into the folds of his jalabah to unleash the serpent as the notes from a flute encourages the cobra to rise from his basket. She began rocking the monster up and down to the same rhythm as the tattooed girl and those men at the same time as if linked on a circuit board launched their stuff over the writhing bodies of those on the bed, great spurts of semen that blinded my eyes, went up my nose and in my mouth. It was like being baptized.

Someone opened a magnum of champagne with an explosive pop and the bubbly stuff cleared the gunk from my eyes and slipped deliciously into my mouth. With my lips stretched open for more, the great heaving mount of the older woman, the one without bonds, lowered over my face. It was like being a bear in a cartoon putting your head in a jar of honey, the sweet sticky stuff covering my chin, my neck, my breasts. She tired of me and moved on to Milly, bending forward at the same time to nurse a stray erection emerging from the mass of limbs and torsos, male bodies and female bodies in one erotic display like a painting depicting the bacchanal that emerged in Rome 200 years before Christ and in which it was the female who ruled. As it should be. And would be again, I thought. It was the best time ever to be alive and best still being born female.

Girls everywhere were growing more comfortable and confident exhibiting their curves, their chic, their nudity. Heels were higher. Clothes were tighter. Breasts were everywhere, and thighs, too, and backs and bare tummies. Even newsreaders are chosen for the cut of their cheekbones, the mystery of their cleavage, their unreserved sensuality. The pretty young blondes are easing out the grey men in grey suits with their deep, doom-laden voices as those in charge of the media, those masters of the air waves, come to see that news of war and chaos is sweetened when read through cupid lips.

What the men of the New World understand, what I was beginning to understand, is simply this: that nothing matters. Nothing. Just this one moment in time and how you best spend it. People are born, they live, they die and the wheel keeps turning. Banks crash and people starve. Empires rise and empires fall. Our time is brief and fragile. If we strip away our garments with our self-doubt and self-imposed morality, what's left is a round room of many mirrors where people can be themselves.

The bacchanal was banned in Rome by the petty politicians who had not been invited to take part. People loathe seeing others enjoy themselves, and condemn others for the very things they most wish to do themselves. For 2000 years, our sexuality has been repressed. For 2000 years, women have been made to feel ashamed of their natural urges, their natural instincts, their desire for multiple partners and that inimitable freedom only found in the hedonistic heat of the orgy. That was going to change. It was changing. There was a revolution going on and I wanted to be out in front of the charge waving the banner.

I heard the shrill ripping of the air behind me and turned my head to watch as two men brought their leather belts down on the perky bottoms of the twins, their wrists hooked to rings set invisibly in the mirror walls. Their bodies moved like sublime snakes as the pain and pleasure blazed up their long spines. The men beat them mercilessly, the girls cried in ecstasy and the two men like rampant fauns set about filling their backsides, their fiery cocks demanding attention after the stimulation of the beating.

Other girls, girls I hadn't seen before, were leaning across the mass of bodies on the bed, their legs spread, the masters of the universe piercing them back and front. More champagne showered over me. Over us all. We were one. I was drunk and delirious. Time was suspended. The temperature had risen. Every space in the round room filled, the white bed raised above the black carpeted floor in an eruption of naked flesh. I sucked and I fucked. I took one cock and two and three and four. My skin was alive and electric with new sensations, coated with semen, girl discharge and sweat.

For a girl, sex is at the heart of our nature, it is our pleasure and deepest desire. For a man, more than pleasure, more than a sense of conquest, sex is a fantasy. The moment a man vanishes inside a woman, he is free from the chains of squalid reality. If he is going to stay one step ahead of reality, he must emerge from that woman and disappear into the next. The fantasy must be kept alive by changing constantly, changing partners and having partners adapt and change through costume and mask, something I had yet to see in Black Spires but felt intuitively would come before I had served out my thirty-one days.

In that marvelous mirror ball where you didn't know which body belonged to whom, your sense of self was lost in a whirlpool of sweating, throbbing flesh, each sensation fading into a new sensation and taking you deeper and deeper, higher and higher, until you became one with the whole. In a world of theories, equations and math, small amounts of matter can contain mega amounts of energy. The orgy is the centrifuge that refines and enriches the life force. Your own pleasure and energy is multiplied to infinity by the vicarious pleasure of those around you.

The temperature had gone up a few more degrees, the lights were low and the moon's silver glow through the high arched windows gave those tumbling, frolicking bodies the look of ghosts and spirits, of satyrs and elves. I watched the men and girls matched in every conceivable way, and in ways beyond conception, exploring and exploiting the supreme pleasures of each other. Men were spanking girls. Girls were spanking girls, kissing girls, licking out girls in one orifice while the other was filled by a passing cock still with enough energy to stay upright and, of course, when it comes to group sex, women have far greater capacity than men; men grow flaccid and tired while women just get more randy.

The men in the mirror room could do anything, and what they wanted to do was be with each other and be with us, the girls with the gift in the house of mirrors. I was overcome with a sense of unfettered joy. Any girl can be an accountant. Any girl can get a first at the LSE. Any girl can get a boyfriend, get engaged, get married, be as the cows and zebras and continue the species. You had to be special to be there at Black Spires and I felt special taking part in that carnival of euphoria and delight. The round room was a circus ring without a ringmaster, anarchic, debauched, perfect.

Every scene in every act unwound and ended. The men in the room were exhausted, drunk, slowly losing themselves to sleep. I, on the other hand, was fully awake, my body burning like a bright light. I had, as Milly had said, been born with the gift and realised that moment that everything that I may achieve in my life would be less from my own efforts than from nurturing that gift.

I had watched through the hours for Simon Roche to appear in the round room and now he did appear, fully dressed, tall and stern, his dark eyes finding me where I had been all that time, in the centre of the large bed, in the centre of the room, in the centre of the activity.

He remained in the doorway and, as he beckoned, I realised that this was the moment I had been waiting for.

Reviews for The Gift of Girls

"Chloe Thurlow's story is top notch and will get you in the mood to agree to anything just to get a slice of what Magdalena has, whether or not you are that way inclined."
ANGELIKA DEVLYN, ALTERNATIVE-READ.COM

"Magdalena is in deep trouble. She has been caught embezzling thousands of pounds from her boss Simon. Desperate to avoid prosecution, she agrees to become his slave for a month. During that time, she will be spanked, cropped, caned and humiliated. She will be penetrated, not only by Simon, but by others – many others. When she becomes one of two women and four men…in bed together, she learns what a truly wanton slut she has become."
QSM – QUALITY SM

"I thought this book was disgusting, but I couldn't put it down and read in three times."

ALLIE HART, AMAZON.COM

"Thievery, promiscuity and (soft) slavery all feature in this…latest addition to Chloe's repertoire…it will be sure to keep active imaginations working overtime and the blood flowing to the most sensual organs of the body for many hours to come."
CARRIE WHITE – SQUIDOO.COM

This final extract is from *Girl Trade,* my most recent novel, published by Xcite in 2011. This was my first experiment in what I call travel erotica, a genre where the writer has the opportunity to describe a journey both in terms of outer surfaces and inner feelings and intuitions.

Back-cover blurb:

Emily dumps her dull boyfriend and takes a holiday alone in Spain.

Captured by people smugglers, she is sold to an Arab Sheikh who teaches her on a sea voyage along the coast of Africa the pleasures of sex, subservience and bondage.

Stolen from the Sheikh's harem, Emily is used and abused by the camel traders who lead her across the Sahara to the slave market in Timbuktu, where she is sold to a black magic ring who practice human sacrifice ... was she only ever a plaything to be discarded, or will the Sheikh arrive in time to save her? This new novel by Chloe Thurlow is a fusion of erotica and travel which further develops the writer's growing reputation.

Slave Girl

All night my body trembled with fever. I was in a sweat, my mind blank, my flesh sizzling as the indigo dye burned indelibly in a line from my chin to my sore naked pussy.

All next day, I was shaking with chills. As I watched the shadows inching around the walls, the contentment I'd felt as Amatullah put the final touches to the spider slipped into despair and melancholy. I had an intuition, a sixth sense, that something terrible was going to happen, that my being branded wasn't the beginning of something but the end. The shadows conjured up an army of dark figures coming to carry me into exile. I was Juliet pining for my Romeo and saw our love ending in poison and death.

Maysoon sat beside the bed. She brought me food, dates, cashews, soups made from spices, sweet balls of rice with sesame. I had an emptiness inside. I tried to eat, but had no appetite, no energy. The girl held my hand and stroked my hair. The pain of those million pinpricks was constant but bearable and I was overcome by a growing sense of misery and loss.

My desire to have Samir inside me was an ague; a craving. I had a cramp in my womb, a sensation that was both unsettling and exhilarating. The fever returned when I slept. I tossed and turned and in my nightmares I was lost in the desert, a barren plateau in every direction; I was on a train racing over a bridge without tracks; I saw myself falling and felt saddened when I realized with horror that I was pregnant, my belly swollen like ripe fruit, a bottomless pit awaiting below my churning arms.

I awoke perspiring with a hollow tummy and a yearning to have the sheikh's children. I wanted lots of them, handsome boys with shiny eyes and girls who would wear the blue tattoo. In my dream, I saw us walking together as a family, not in the coastal town beyond the fort, but in London, along Sloane Street and Knightsbridge.

It took many days for the marks to heal. My chin was bruised and there were scabs in a line down my chest. I couldn't see the spider clutching my pubic area. The wound was covered in a mottled carapace like the shell of a tortoise. It stung when I peed. I gritted my teeth and tears sprang to my eyes. Maysoon wiped away the drips with her fingertips and I felt nostalgic for those sweltering afternoons squirting in playful fountains into the air. Time is relentless, always racing. The past withers the moment the page turns.

The light in the arched windows above my bed grew less harsh and the oven heat of the tower lessened as August must have drifted into autumn and I imagined the trees in the garden at home turning into a quilt of russet and gold.

When I asked Maysoon where Samir had gone, she shrugged as if such things were not her concern. She threw up her fine shoulders and smiled, her lips turning into a bow, her white teeth framing the little pink tongue that had impelled me to edge of delirium. While I had not lost the custom of thinking about the future, Maysoon was fixed in the moment, to the urges of her body and passing desires.

I couldn't help wondering what Maysoon would do when she were old, when her flesh lost its sweet smell and suppleness. But the girl seemed to have been born knowing that the future we imagine is abstract, unreal, the false God that makes us sacrifice present joys for illusory far greater joys at some unspecified time. It is this attitude that makes us build careers, invest, save for pensions, rejecting the day for the gnomes of tomorrow.

Maysoon hooked her fingers about my lips to force out a smile. She ran her hand through the air, showing me a boat at sea, her mime confirming my guess that the sheikh was taking the Indian man and the other immigrants I had met to the Canary Islands to begin a new life. We are all nomads, each one of us eternally making our way home. The girl danced. She kissed my lips, her long black hair tickling my breasts. She ate the food I didn't eat and left with the empty bowls to join the activity and gossip among the women.

One of Scheherazade's stories is about a small animal that lived at the top of a tower in a state of lethargy and awoke when someone climbed the stairs. Like the chameleons that basked in the sun on the fortress walls, the creature had the ability to light up and changed color as the steps drew closer. The story defined me those long days without Samir. Each time I heard the sound of the door opening and closing, the swish of robes along the walkway with its earthenware tiles patterned with brick-red spiders, the spider between my legs pulsed with life as if my lover had finally come.

My mind healed as the scabs fell away, but that feeling that my future was uncertain remained, a pain only the sheikh could heal. I hungered for him and feared he would never come and came to see that fear and arousal are patterns on the same piece of cloth.

The door was no longer locked. I could escape. But why would I? Where would I go? I was no longer a nomad. I was home, a child in a diaphanous dress that billowed about me as I explored the fort's many corridors and hidden rooms; they were endless, a maze, and sometimes I became lost and had to wind my way back through the labyrinth like Ariadne after slaying the Minotaur. Some of the rooms must have been empty for many years, and there were rooms below ground with the cold chill of things best forgotten.

The two old men who had been infuriated when I first arrived with the sheikh followed my every move with glaucoma-dulled eyes, watching me as if I were a cuckoo hatching from a parakeet's nest. I watched them chewing on wads of beetel, spitting, kicking up eddies of dust as they shuffled away. I would scurry off on bare feet to join the women on hot afternoons when they sat in the shade under the colonnade in the courtyard making jewellery.

They threaded silver chains with turquoise and coral, amber and desert jade, their creations all the more remarkable because they were put away and never worn. The women clucked their tongues as they talked. I understood what they were saying but not always what they meant. I had learned Arabic like a child by listening. The women laughed and corrected my pronunciation, their words like lines of poetry with a distinctive metre, a rhythm, a subtlety. Their words were a libretto. A continuum. Like time. It was passing. Another sunset. Another sunrise. Another day without Samir.

It was early morning, cool still. I was in the kitchen, filling my belly, and watched as Amatullah and Yasmeen filled three baskets with necklaces and bracelets.

There was an air of excitement all through the fort. Traders with pack animals and colorful costumes had appeared from the south. Yasmeen told me they came every year and the caravanserai became raucous with the snorts and whinnies of camels and horses, the snake charmer playing a flute, the sound of a hammer beating a metal pots, the press of people enjoying the cool now the hot months were passing.

Did I look sad and lost? I'm sure I did.

'Chengi, you come,' Amatullah said.

I pointed to myself.

'Me?' I asked.

She looked around the room as if searching for someone who wasn't there, then smiled. 'Yes, girl, you,' she said and my heart swelled in my chest.

'*Ma'assalama.*'

Thank you, I said.

Amatullah threw up her hands to show there was no need for thanks. I was one of them, a woman among women. To hide my hair, they dressed me in a blue quilted burkha and I carried the third basket out into the crowds.

Amatullah and Yasmeen were calm, unruffled women who moved through the fortress like shadows. But when they bartered with the merchants, they metamorphosed into harpies, raising their fists, cackling and hollering, parting with the trinkets as if those necklaces and bracelets were glued to the baskets in which they lay wrapped in muslin cloths. In contrast, their quick fingers grasped for the goods they were taking in exchange – saffron, worth its weight in gold, Yasmeen said; rugs from Persia, shimmering bolts of fabric from Pakistan, bush meat packed in salt from Kenya, live birds from faraway jungles, foods for a feast I assumed was to celebrate the return of Samir.

I had made a vow long ago never to wear knickers again and, except for the St Christopher on a thong around my neck, I wore nothing beneath the burkha. My head was covered and my kohl-farded eyes were hidden behind a mesh. The area below my bottom lip was itchy and it seemed as if the thread was stretching as the blue spider awoke from its slumbers and slid down into the furrowed lips of my vagina. My throat was dry. My breath came in short gasps. The earthy smells of men and animals made me wet and feverish.

A plump, bare-headed Arab in a dusty white kaftan was beating the flanks of a donkey with a whip, the sound of those lashes like a piece of music once loved and heard again unexpectedly. He leaned back, flexing his arm and, as the leather snapped, I felt a tingle down my spine. My palms were damp. My back was running with sweat and I felt breathless as

I recalled the tongue of the whip crossing my bare flesh on the boat, the sheikh extinguishing the fire with his tongue, the stripes I wore with pride and which healed all too quickly. There is something unutterably arousing being hidden in veils, something masochistic, yet perverted, and my desire for the sheikh became so intense I felt a trickle of drool slip down my thigh.

I didn't realize I had come to a complete halt. I had closed my eyes and saw myself in the cabin at sea, my fingers clenched around the porthole, my backside baring the marks of the cane administered by the mechanic. I remembered the feeling of relief as I bent forward, curling my toes, gritting my teeth, the snakebite of the sheikh's short-handled whip searing my spread cheeks, that alchemical miracle of pain turning to pleasure as the lines of fire sizzled across my astonished bottom. Six times the lash came down and with the seventh my fate was sealed, I was purified, consecrated as the sheikh's concubine.

My knees trembled. Moisture was gathering between my legs and around the tops of my thighs.

The plump man must have known I was a girl who enjoyed the taste of the whip. He had stopped flogging the donkey. When I opened my eyes, he was standing close to me staring through the mesh screen into my yearning soul, my unquenchable thirsts. He ran the tips of his podgy fingers over the lash he was holding and grinned a mouthful of red-stained teeth. That man wanted to beat me and it was terrifying to realize that I wanted to be beaten. It was discipline that I needed, and it was this deficiency since the sheikh had left that had found me mournful and melancholic. I was a slave to my own primal hungers. I could take the whip but would never be tamed. This was my weakness and my strength. You are what you think. Be yourself and try to be happy. But first, be yourself.

Odd phrases as if from some other world fluttered like pennants in my confused mind. The spider was moving. My pussy was sodden. My mouth had fallen open.

'Assalamu alaikum.'

God be with you, the man said, our momentary connection making me feel as if I were standing there stark naked.

My throat tightened with anguish and I would have remained rooted to the spot had Yasmeen not grabbed my hand and pulled me away.

'Tut, tut, tut, Chengi,' she said, and I realized Yasmeen was wiser than I had thought, that she had been privy to my hysterical musings, that my tendency to underestimate people was, as Mummy said, my Achilles' heel.

We hurried back into the fort, our baskets filled. Being out in the world, even for that short time, was invigorating. I was a vampire with a transfusion of fresh blood. Those days of doubt had slipped back beneath the surface of things. I climbed the stairs with a silver tureen I found in the kitchen. I sat outside the stone shower, leaned against the battlements, the sun dipping in the east over the sea, and studied in the fading light the spider's reflection in the shiny sides of the bowl.

By raising my chin and pulling on the thread, by flexing and contracting my vagina muscles, I could urge the spider to go up on all eight legs. I could make it move one way, then the other, and I could imagine nothing more erotic than Samir's resolute cock parting the eight dancing legs and feeding the ravenous creature the spider was guarding.

The tattoo branded me as a member of the clan and protected the clan's possessions. I was a part of something. I belonged. I shook myself like a puppy running out of the sea and, with an intake of breath, a sigh of relief, a moan that glided up from my chest, I slid forward, my legs spread. My pussy was a lake. My clit throbbed, smarted, vibrated like a bell that rang out the message that I had been neglecting this little fount of all pleasure.

It had been weeks since I had last had an orgasm. The sight and sound of the lash in the caravanserai had reminded me of who I was, what I needed. I stroked the spider. I found the pumping heart of its hidden eye and coated the bowl I was holding with a squirt of creamy warm broth that gushed out of me like nectar from an exotic fruit, waves of luscious discharge thick as milk from a cow.

If only men knew!

That night after we ate, our bellies engorged, Maysoon and I danced. The women had made me a costume like that which I had seen the girl wearing the night I came to the fort, the same close-fitting cap fringed with pearls that covered her face in a constantly moving veil, the same arrangement of beads looped in strings across her torso in such a way that, as she danced, so her breasts were alternatively covered and uncovered; the green gemstone sparkling in her navel above the diaphanous curtain of her low slung skirt that revealed and concealed her sex as her belly gyrated, the lush dome of golden flesh like a rising sun that mesmerized the men gathered about the fire.

Never before had I seen anything so sensual, so erotic, so arousing. Now, I, too could dance the dance. I had those weeks learned from Maysoon how to grind my hips and rotate my distended belly, nurtured during those days of indolence. My limbs were long, my body unblemished except for the mark, as white as candlewax now that I had spent so much time in the shade.

Maysoon hummed a tune and we moved in perfect rhythm, ivory and golden, like two queens from an extravagant chess set. We danced until we were breathless, we shed our costumes and the taste of her warm brine in my mouth that night was an elixir, a magic potion, the antidote to the poison Juliet had so foolishly gulped down her throat.

I could have sucked the girl dry. I could with concentration, with Zen will, have transformed into the spider and built my web in the grotto of her sweet humid sex. My clitoris, awakened earlier in the day, stood rigid in the bonnet of my coral inner lips, the channel of my vagina flooding with hot girlsperm as Maysoon's tongue squirmed like a flame rising from a bonfire. The girl was tireless, a clockwork ballerina in a newly-wound music box. I could have bathed in her gaping mouth until the light of dawn lit the arched windows. I could have drifted to infinity and it took all my resolve to stop myself.

I was saving myself. The girl was the hors d'oevre, the *tapas*, not the feast. The women had been running around in a tizz all day cleaning pots, beheading chickens, washing salt from bush meat, stirring date juice into the flour they fed in flattened patties into the conical oven, removing the piping discs of pita as they puffed up like engorged vagina lips, licking their burnt fingertips, their faces glowing and damp.

The night turned black. I slept without dreaming and awoke like a little girl on Christmas morning.

How brilliant for the sheikh to go when he did and return when I was ready for him. My belly that had grown rotund and voluptuous was adorned with a green stone, shiny as an emerald, the color of my eyes. I watched from the ramparts an hour after sunrise as an open-backed pickup crossed the desert from town. They must have come straight from the boat and I knew, somehow I knew, that the vehicle carried Samir, Mohammed, Azar and Umah. They shot by the caravanserai, the driver tooted his horn as he swerved through the gate and they vanished from view in a cloud of dust.

I should have gone down to the courtyard with the other women. That was my place, my role, to throw up my hands, to fall to the floor and weep. But I remained in the tower, the creature from Scheherazade's story. I had a new life, I liked my new life, but I knew from my old life that just as absence warms the heart, so denial keens the appetite. When Samir climbed the stairs and I finally heard his robes sweep along the corridor, he would be ready for me and I would light up and glow like a chameleon.

I didn't have long to wait. He appeared in the doorway and I ran into his arms. He had remembered how to kiss and when he kissed my insatiable lips all the air gushed from my body. He carried me to the stone shower where I washed away the dust of his journey and he washed away the dust of my doubts and despair. I could smell the sea on his skin. His face was bronzed, flawless as a God. His cock stood between us and, when I bent to take it into my throat, I felt complete, a lock being joined by the key to paradise.

Samir's warm manhood was an alien sun that energized me. His taste was sugary like sherbet. I felt spasms rolling down from his ribbed stomach and paused, not wanting that first orgasm to come too quickly. I rose with a long wet lick from his curly-covered balls to the groove in his soft helmet, from his navel to the broad plain of his smooth hairless chest. I climbed up into his embrace and the little sheikh throbbed against my belly.

He pushed the plug back in the shower. We dripped in the morning sun. The yellow parakeets stood in a line, hopping from foot to foot, close enough to touch, and sang their dissonant song.

'You are happy to see me, habibi?' he said.

'So happy, you can't imagine,' I answered, careful with every word, and he leaned back, pleased and surprised.

'You speak my language?'

I ran my forefinger in a line from my chin to the spider. 'I had a good teacher,' I told him.

He went down on his haunches to admire Amatullah's handiwork. He caressed my mount. 'It's beautiful,' he said.

'And you are beautiful.'

'Yes, me beautiful.' He kissed the spider. 'She beautiful.'

'You speak my language,' I said and he looked up over my round belly, which he stroked.

We entered the tower. The light was hazy, like a dream. I took his hand and kissed his palm. I sucked his fingers, one after the other, then slid like an obedient slave over the pillows piled high on the dais of carpets. I got a good purchase with my knees, my breasts hung like udders over my lovely tummy and, as I rolled my hips seductively, an ancient memory flooded my mind. I was thirteen in the showers after a hockey match at school, a skinny thing with budding breasts barely contouring my chest. A plump hirsute girl ripe as a peach slapped my backside with a wet towel and all the girls laughed when she roared 'shame your ass is your best feature'.

I was angry and tearful, but the memory now brought a smile to my lips. The hairy girl may have been right. My bottom was full, plump, two precise domes that rang out like a bell as the weathered hand I'd kissed came down in a hard smack that set me on the yellow brick road to euphoria. The weight of that slap pushed me forward, collapsing the pile of cushions, and without my arms for support, I buried my head and pushed the target up to meet the next stroke of discipline.

There is nothing but nothing like a good spanking. I wiggled all the more as my bum grew redder, sweat poured from me like a tide and the sheikh's wet hand rang out louder and louder as smack after glorious smack rained down on my intoxicated posterior. I liked the whip. You can enjoy the cane. But your lover's hand is the fleshly connection of your lover, it is his penis in another form. Men with large hands are endowed with large cocks and the sheikh's hands were long and fine. If you look at the shape of a man's palm and the soft curve of a girl's backside you can see that they are meant to join. They are the two parts of a child's first puzzle. All through my childhood Daddy had said what I needed was a 'damn good spank'. How prophetic.

I wriggled and writhed. My breasts wobbled. My wet hair hung in a golden veil over my eyes. Samir beat me until the glow spread up my back and down my thighs. He beat me until my drenched pussy sent a stream of boiling lava down the insides of my legs. He beat me until the smell of my arousal stewed his mind and he fell on me like a satyr, driving his spear deep into my winking backside, filling me to the rim and we exploded instantly roaring like beasts.

We lay in a lake of sticky fluids, chests beating, the light growing stronger as he revived sufficiently to swivel around and investigate the tattoo. He licked the eight legs of the spider, he petted and nudged my swollen clit and his tongue like a sword slid into the sheath of my flooded vagina.

All warm and soft, the little sheikh was perfumed with my own scents as it worked between my teeth and, like baking clay, slowly hardened. Is there anything better than sucking a man's cock after it has rutted your backside? Is there anything better than fucking?

The morning was soon gone and Samir was gone all too soon. We bathed away the juice coating our bodies and he threw a sheet around his waist. As he hurried along the walkway, the parakeets took wing and suddenly, for no reason, a cold chill like a bad omen ran down my spine.

He vanished with a wave through the open door and I shook the feeling off. I had been looking into the future. There is no future. I told myself there is only this moment, the aroma of food slowly cooking, rising up the fortress walls, and Maysoon must have guessed I was starving because she appeared with a warm clay bowl and a crispy pita rolled up like a cigar between her pouting lips. There were slices of meat with secret blends of spices on a bed of chutney made from mangoes mixed with pitted dates and brown rice. We ate with our fingers and wiped the bowl clean with pita strips that smelled of the oven.

We grinned and gazed into each other's eyes as we ate and the joy I felt from the sheikh coming home was doubled because in Maysoon there was no resentment or jealousy. He had come to me. Perhaps another time he would first go to her, and I would remember. I would carry her food without doubt or antipathy. I would learn grace and equanimity, the laws of the harem, the law of life.

We dressed and practised our belly dance. As the heat faded, we stripped and lay in each other's arms, the light in the twelve arched windows blushing a delectable shade of pink. Before we dressed for my début, Maysoon painted my eyes in kohl, my lips with a scarlet dye that Yasmeen ground from red petals and paste; she rubbed cream over my chin and down the silken strand to my pubis. In the shadowy light, the thread turned silver and the spider sparkled. More than anything I would have loved to have been in possession of a full-length mirror so that I could have locked that moment into the vaults of my memory.

147

We were ready. I could hear the musicians in the courtyard below. I wanted to go down and join the festivities, but Maysoon held me back.

'No, no, Chengi. Have patience.'

She had said this to me before, many times, and it was so hard to learn.

She was standing beside the battlements gazing out in the direction of town. I joined her and we stared through the fading light until a spiral of dust appeared on the horizon. The spiral grew larger, turning like a corkscrew. I heard the purr of powerful engines as three black-windowed vehicles crossed the desert like a line of scarabs. Their approach seemed slow but then, as they drew closer, the engines roared and the brakes squealed as they turned towards the fort and disappeared into the gates.

'They have come,' Maysoon said.

'Who?'

She looked surprised. 'The Emir,' she replied. 'The Emir is here.'

'The Emir?'

She nodded and in her eyes were two crescents of moonlight. Maysoon didn't elaborate. I practiced patience.

Above us, the night sky had never been so low and imposing. Green and blue and orange shooting stars crisscrossed the firmament below the slowly turning constellations. I stood in my costume, my ompholus, gateway to my womb, bejewelled in a gleaming green stone, a third eye, deep and unseeing.

It was time to go. Maysoon drew the cap over my head and tucked my golden hair below the intricate weaving of white pearls. We touched lips, careful not to smear the greasepaint, and she ran the tip of her tongue over my teeth.

'I love you, Chengi,' she said, a rare...no, not rare, a unique show of affection and friendship that made a tear well into the corner of my eye.

The Fifty Shades of Grey Phenomena

'I love you, Maysoon.'

She grinned and I understood, suddenly I understood: when she was old and no longer desirable, I would be the same. I would love her as she loved me. We would buy spices when the traders came from the south. We would embellish other girls with the blue tattoo and they would with their hedonism and lascivious responsibilities maintain an air of peace and order.

As we made our way down the two flights of stairs, everything about me was swaying, my skirts of chiffon, the beadwork top, the veil of pearls hiding but not quite hiding my face. Everything about me, about the two of us, was tempting, ripe, a feast for a feast. If a girl has a moment when she is at her best, this was my moment. My limbs were long and slender, my bottom tingled, my feet glided silently on the stone stairs, my belly was gorgeously rounded, a marble dome that by some genius of geometry had swelled in a curve that reached to the same vertical point as my breasts that were full and perky with nipples hard as nuggets of gold.

We entered the colonnade with its row of tables laden with rich smelling platters and tureens. The compound was lit by flaming braziers on tall metal posts and a pair of sheep turned on the spit over the fire. The women fluttered by on hennaed feet in new dresses bringing bowls with dips and baskets of pita, filling every space until the tables groaned with the weight of the feast.

The men had gathered in concentric circles according to rank. Behind their chatter the musicians plucked and hammered their instruments, lutes, a zither they call a *qanun*, a tambourine, reed pipes, tablas of varying shapes and sizes, their rhythms slow with an emotive power that made my fingers and toes tingle.

Samir was dressed in white with a white turban held by a single band. Beside him sat the Emir, all in black with a black turban decorated with four bands of gold that I assumed marked his status as the blue spider marked my own.

'That's the Emir?' I whispered.

Maysoon nodded.

'He is related to Samir?'

She looked back at me as if I were simple. 'He is the head of the tribe,' she said. 'The sheikh's father.'

I looked again. Of course Samir was the man's son. They had the same shiny dark eyes, the same high cheek bones and carved features, the Emir's face masked by a heavy moustache and beard that clung tightly to his chin. They were the same height, but the Emir was broader and had about him the air of a tyrant.

Hanif, all in white like Samir, sat at Samir's left, and behind them were men in black and the two old men who never left the fort. Azar, Mohammed and Umah were part of the larger outer circle, a place for everyone and everyone in their place.

The women led by Amatullah emerged in a line with bowed heads and the first tantalizing platters of food. The men took bowls and filled them. The women scurried off again. It all seemed well-organized, rehearsed, as the girl and I had rehearsed our belly dance.

No sooner had the women disappeared than they reappeared with more courses, the smells filling the air with mystery and promise. The men grew louder, the beat of the music faster, drawing me hypnotically behind Maysoon as she wafted out from under the colonnade, her body like a snake weaving ancient patterns of sensuality and seduction. Like a shadow, I followed every move, every step, every gyration, excitement growing in me like fire. To dance in this way before the ravenous eyes of a sea of men is the ultimate turn on, to be desired unconditionally, universally, is the feminine ideal, the heart of our role, ultimate bliss.

My eyelashes, heavy with kohl, fluttered like two tiny birds. I didn't so much see as perceive the Emir coming to his feet. He was motionless for a moment, then moved at speed, three steps and he reached the musicians. I didn't know what was happening. He kicked the tabla from beneath the drummer's hands, the instrument rolled across the dirt and the music hushed to silence as if plunging into the void.

The world stood still. The Emir grabbed my hand and pulled me under the light of the nearest brazier. I noticed Samir leap to his feet and race towards us, but he was too late. His father tore off my cap and threw it on the floor. He stared into my eyes. He ripped the beads covering my breasts and the skirt from my hips.

As Samir reached him, the Emir stood back, staring at me and holding off his son. The men of the first circle and the men in black gathered about us. They were silent as the Emir studied the blue tattoo. His eyes ran up the silken thread to the silver St Christopher glowing in the firelight.

He looked finally into my eyes and in his expression I saw the contempt powerful men in poor countries feel for the colonial, for the big corporations, for the western governments who for five hundred years have exploited the people in his world. The Christian symbol at my throat represented everything he despised. His hand like a claw reached out and ripped the thong from my neck. He threw the medal to the floor and ground it into the dust with the heel of his leather boot.

As he turned to Samir, two of the black turbaned men grabbed my arms. The Emir hit Samir, only once, a thunderous blow across the side of his face, knocking him off his feet.

'Fool,' he cried.

Samir stood. The tic on his neck was vibrating, but he wasn't afraid.

'She is mine, Father, mine,' he yelled.

The Emir waved his arm. 'She is from out there,' he screamed. 'You defile our land.'

'She is a woman. She is my woman. She belongs to me.'

'Nothing belongs to you. Have I taught you nothing. Everything belongs to the tribe.'

'But Father, I want her…'

'You are not a child, Samir. We cannot have whatever we want.'

He ran at his father and grabbed the folds of his black tunic.

'I will not give her up, Father. I will never give her up,' he said.

His voice was low, considered. In the moment's silence I thought for one optimistic breath that the Emir was going to relent. I was wrong. He unscrewed Samir's hands from his clothes.

'Take him away,' he ordered.

Three men grabbed the sheikh from behind.

'Father, I will not give her up. It is my right.'

'My son, you have no rights. You have responsibilities.'

The men in black hauled Samir towards the steps beneath the colonnade. He was shouting, screaming oaths. Black tears running with kohl streamed down my face.

The Emir turned back to me and spat on the ground, the spray touching my feet.

Yasmeen came forward with a robe she wrapped it around my shoulders. As the men urged me across the courtyard, she bent swiftly, retrieved the St Christopher and pushed it into my palm.

One of the men grabbed an oil lamp and I was hurried down the steps to the cellars I had explored during my long wait for Samir. I was shoved into the first cell. The man leading the way placed the lamp in the corner and I was grateful for the light that he left behind, for this mote of human kindness. The door closed behind them and I heard the metallic rasp of the bolt sliding into place.

There was no escape. I wilted into the straw mattress and wept the night through. Were they going to kill me? Behead me? Cut me in pieces and feed me to the jackals? All night I lay without sleep clutching the St Christopher waiting to find out.

Reviews for Girl Trade

"The way the descriptions are presented made my imagination complete. Thurlow should be applauded for her exquisite creativity with Girl Trade. Never in all the hundreds and thousands of romance tales and stories that I have read over the decades has a novel left me so speechless."
> BRYNN CARSON, SIMPLY EROTIC REVIEWS

"There's more than a hint of swashbuckling about this book's cover and sure enough it tells the tale of a diplomat's spoiled daughter who is kidnapped while holidaying in the Canary Islands. She is taken on an epic journey across the oceans in the company of pirates and smugglers, and to stay alive she must become the perfect concubine. A very readable tale, written by an accomplished author."
> MARKETPLACE

"This novel ought to have a six star rating, it was that amazing. For all mature women – a must. The end of this novel was so emotional and consuming. I read the last 15% in one sitting!"
> XENI – GOODREADS

"Chloe Thurlow is fast becoming my favorite writer. No-one writes erotica as if its a 'proper' book, except for Chloe ...an excellent story...with steamy interludes as our heroine gets up to her naughty tricks."
> AMY – GOODREADS.COM

"I did not know this was an erotica book until the end. Oops! But it was deliciously naughty and left me blushing page after page."
> LAURIE BOETTCHER, GOODREADS.COM

PART 5

Erotic Articles

The three essay/articles that follow deal with different aspects of erotica.

Erotica For Beginners, published on the reader/reviewer network Goodreads.com, explores some of the themes contained in Part 1 of this book

Shades of James: What Publishers Want looks at what publishers are seeking in the wake of EL James's success. It first appeared on Goodreads.

The Body Stripper Bare looks at erotica in art and photography. The article was first published in the magazine *The New Nude,* reproduced here with permission from Hegre-Art.com.

Erotica for Beginners

There are three reasons for having sex: reproduction, cash and pleasure.

Pleasure to remain pleasurable must be constantly nourished and renewed. The French call the orgasm *la petite mort*, the little death that announces, not the height of pleasure, but pleasure's end. To prolong and enhance pleasure, we have the erotic. What does erotic mean and what's the difference between erotic and pornographic?

A pornographic photograph is designed to encourage sexual desire. An erotic photograph captures an erotic situation. A man watching a woman turn to study the ladder in her stockings can be far more seductive than the wanton nude gazing at the camera lens. The erotic contains an aesthetic quality that stimulates the mind as well as the body.

The erotic may end in orgasm, but strives for fulfillment by reaching for darker more complex spheres of pleasure: deferral, anticipation, transgression, costumes, role play. Erotic sex consists of opening a windowless door and entering a black room, probably masked, not knowing what you are going to find.

In Quentin Tarantino's 'Pulp Fiction', John Travolta as Vincent Vega asks Jody, Rosanna Arquette, why she has a stud in her tongue. 'For oral stimulation,' she replies. Jody puts up with the discomfort of wearing the stud for the gratification of her boyfriend. Her pleasure derives from giving pleasure.

But it is not a one way street. With skilful artifice: makeup, tattoos, piercings, hints of nudity – breasts, legs, shoulder blades – a woman in making herself an object of desire inspires passion and creativity. Like the artist's muse, her apparent position of submission, or inferiority, to man is similarly her domination, or mastery, over man. A show of obedience is only show and can equally create a sense of liberation, a sense that one is obeying their own instincts.

An experiment at Cambridge University in the UK showed that when numerous metronomes were placed on a stage and set off at different times, in a short period, they start to beat together. They are not individuals, but ciphers connected by the rhythms of all and everything about them.

We all have a dark side, mysterious places hidden even to ourselves. Erotica allows us to look at that side, to break the bonds of our conditioning, to cease beating in time to all the other metronomes and to set out on the search for the greater joy that comes with self-knowledge. If that all sounds terrifying, for beginners we have erotic literature.

The first rule of the erotic is the aesthetic quality: erotic literature has to be literate. Through the pages of well-written erotica, authors take us into the minds and bodies and fantasies of their characters in the privacy and comfort of our own little beds before turning out the night light and drifting into our dreams.

Shades of James: What Publishers Want

If you look at publishers' guidelines, what they are all looking for is 'great stories'. Hollywood producers have the same hunger. They want to get their hands on a great script. What they mean by a great script is a script that's virtually the same as the script that turned into the biggest box office success the previous year. They want it to be different, but just a bit different. That's why producers, and publishers, like sequels.

Publishers are more daring than filmmakers; its costs less to publish a book than make a film. But, at heart, they are just as conventional. The success of *Fifty Shades of Grey* and its spin offs has whetted the taste buds for more erotica. But editors are not seeking the extraordinary, the inventive, the original. They want to see stories that are kind of like Fifty Shades, but kind of different. Fifty Shades with vampires? Fifty Shades with an aliens beamed down from a more sassy planet to teach earth women the joys of bondage? Fifty Shades set in the Wild West – *Sexing Texas*, maybe?

The upshot is that erotic authors are obliged to negotiate a highwire suspended between imitating EL James and being so innovative that their precious creation falls into the abyss. The punishing sessions in your novel needs to be harsh, but not brutal; extreme, but not too extreme. Is that two dozen spanks not four dozen? Fur-lined handcuffs? A lifetime supply of witch hazel for those welts and stinging tingles? These questions do not have answers. They are considerations. Mental Post-its.

Next on the wanted list is an appeal for strong, dynamic, intelligent characters that 'readers identify with' and take to their hearts. Mmm? Nabokov's purring sex kitten Lolita? Capote's mesmerizing Holly Golightly? The multifaceted *Jane Eyre* from Charlotte Brontë's pen? Or the unpredictable Cathy from sister Emily's *Wuthering Heights?* You need a touch of all of them, plus a shade of Anastasia Steele, or Bella Swan, an ugly duckling who is beautiful but unaware and far too modest to admit she's beautiful.

The strong female lead will attract the paradoxical but charismatic male: the Sean Connery or Daniel Craig version of James Bond? Indiana Jones, an adventurer professor with mind over muscles. Perhaps someone younger, a Zac Efron lookalike with Taylor Lautner's twinkle. In other words, a cocktail of male perfection with a twist of lemon, what the reader, or viewer, expects, but shot from a different angle.

With the great story, with its twists and obstacles, and great characters, with their thrust and contradictions, editors want to read great sex that arises through plot, not sprinkled in like spice in soup, a good blend of spanking and orgasms, not too much, mind, just enough. They want romance, passion, a sense of redemption and, most of all, tension. Which puts you right back on the highwire.

The Body Stripped Bare

Mankind since time began has been inspired, angered and obsessed by his own naked self.

If exposed before the mirror we see ourselves for what we are, a brief glimpse of our soul, the nude in art is a representation of what we can be, what we strive for. The artist's aspiration to create a surface perfection is, to follow the thesis, merely the visual expression of our own desire to reach inner perfection.

Conservative and liberal thinkers have kept, often violently, to their own sides of the debate, and it is unlikely that a bridge will ever span the torrents raging between them. The discourse, though, belonged historically to a privileged elite until the time of the industrial revolution, when the advent of photography and the mechanical printing press brought nudity to the masses.

Up until then, artists inspired by the nude had drawn traditionally on classical and biblical imagery, as if gilded youth and physical ease belonged always to another time, the far away past, not the real and censorious present. Early

Victorian artists veiled their work in references from mythology and literature, but remained careful to select subjects which conveyed moral or religious undertones: the story of Lady Godiva, who rode naked on a horse through the streets of Coventry as a protest against high taxes; the fauns and fairies frolicking in the woods from Shakespeare's *A Midsummer Night's Dream*; or Diana, the Virgin Goddess of the Hunt, identified with the Virgin in Christian iconography.

Where the nude had become respectable in the rest of Europe, the British were late entrants to the form until a group of progressive young artists in the 1860s crossed the Channel and returned inspired by the work of French neo-classical painters such as Ingres and Gérôme. They were influenced by the spirit of a lost Greek utopia and began presenting figures as compositions in high art, emphasizing classical themes, while elevating style and form above narrative.

It was at this time in British art that Venus appears with fuller proportions as the ideal for natural womanhood, acknowledging woman's traditional biological role, but also suggesting more radical notions of female emancipation. Since Botticelli painted *The Birth of Venus*, artists have returned to the image in constant search of the Renaissance.

Work hung in exhibitions followed codes set down by legislation, but artists were constantly pushing back the boundaries by displaying nude figures in ever more daring arrangements. An important boost to nude freedom came by Royal Appointment: Queen Victoria and Prince Albert not only admired the form, but the Queen made a point of giving her Consort a print of a nude for his birthday each year as a symbol of her love. Private commissions enabled artists to explore personal ways of representing the nude, giving full expression to desires marginalized by the galleries. By the end of the 19th century, the human body in positions of subjection and arousal were making their way into galleries to engage the public more provocatively than ever before.

The development of photography created a new demand for the nude. Easily made prints blurred the boundaries between the real and imagined body and offered a new immediacy not possible in painting. Where the nude had historically formed only one part of the artist's composition, in photography, the representation of the model became an end in itself.

Painters, influenced by this change, began to move away from the conventions of the idealized nude and transferred figures from biblical and classical settings to more contemporary surroundings. French realists Manet and Degas presented the body in seedy domestic interiors that hinted at illicit sexual activity, while British artists placed the nude out of doors to imply the benefits of fresh air, sun bathing and exercise.

As film followed photography as a means to express the nude in art, the censors were still lying in wait with their strictures on what the public should and should not be allowed to see in the privacy of a darkened auditorium. Luis Buñuel and Salvador Dali's 1920s classic *L'Âge d'Or* was banned from public viewing because of its 'subversive eroticism' and the 'furious dissection of civilized values.'

The film vanished for many years, but has since been shown on television and can be viewed at the surrealist galleries at the Tate Modern in London. It was first screened in Britain in 1950, when the sole complaint was from the Royal Society for the Protection of Animals. Bare breasts and a nun being thrown from a window caused no offence, but one of the characters is seen booting a small dog up the backside. Social mores had changed, but not the English.

The debate over nudity and public morals raged across the two sides of the divide throughout the 20th century, and will no doubt even in our more enlightened times continue to do so. At the Super Bowl finals in the United States not so very long ago, Janet Jackson's exposed right breast inspired 200,000 complaints from viewers. That, of course, took no note of the 10 million viewers who may have approved.

Appendix

Once you have completed your novel, don't send the manuscript out randomly. Books that arrive 'over the transom' end up in the literary graveyard, the infamous 'slush pile' – a dusty cupboard in the bad old days, these days a black hole on a junior editors' hard drive.

Start your research with the publishers listed in this appendix – and check them all individually. Publishers come and go, and by the time you are reading this the publisher that seems most suitable may be out of business, or has changed to another specialty. Find out exactly what each individual publishers is looking for and study their guidelines. Exactly 'What Publishers Want' can be found in Part 5, Erotic Articles.

Most publishers ask for a Proposal consisting of three chapters, a one-page synopsis, a more detailed summary of the book, a brief bio of the author, a head and shoulders photograph and details of what you can do to help make your book a success. Have you published other books? Does you sister work as a feature writer on the local newspaper? If you think something may help, throw it in. Generally, publishers do not want cover designs, they have a neaurotic art department to deal with that.

Ensure you own all the rights before you make a submission. For example, if the work has previously been published in book form and is being submitted to a digital publisher, check the original contract to be certain you have the right to do so. Similarly, if at any time you had a collaborator or co-writer on board, make sure their rights are not bring infringed.

Thanks to EL James, publishers are more open to erotic experimentation of every kind. However, there are some fixed ground rules across the industry. Erotica is an adult activity for an adult audience. Sex, in all its moods and seasons, is consensual and participants are <u>always</u> over the age of 18.

Some other no nos.

- No pedophilia, suggestions of pedophilia, allusions to pedophilia.
- No rape or non-consensual violence.
- No necrophilia – that's sex involving the dead.
- No bestiality – sex involving animals.

No blood. Whipping, paddling, strapping, caning, spanking, bondage, gagging and many other types of adult activity have their place on the erotic palette. Bottoms may grow a deep shade of violet, cuffs chaff the wrists, and willow switches may stripe the skin. But never do they break the surface of the skin and draw blood. Discipline is sensual, as well as consensual, an extreme type of foreplay. Even monthly periods, natural and normal in life and in novels, are best ignored in erotica.

Alyson Books

http://www.alyson.com

The Association of Erotic Artists

http://www.associationoferoticartists.com

Circlet Press

http://www.circlet.com

Daedalus Publishing

http://www.daedaluspublishing.com

Ellora's Cave

http://www.jasminejade.com

The Erotic Author's Association

http://www.eroticauthorsassociation.com

Erotic Flash Fiction

http://eroticflashfiction.blogspot.co.uk

Erotic Readers and Writers Association

http://www.erotica-readers.com

Greenery Press

http://www.greenerypress.com

Grove Press

www.groveatlantic.com

Inks Erotica

www.inkserotica.co.uk

Kensington (Brava)

http://www.kensingtonbooks.com

Siren Publishing

http://www.sirenpublishing.com

Laid & Betrayed

Beneath the angelic features of goody, goody Grace Goode is a shameless slut dying to take her clothes off and get spanked. It just needs the right man to say the right words…and Charlie Wright was born with a silver tongue. After being stripped, seduced and spread across the internet for the world to see, Grace hears the call of "cold hard cash" as she sets off on an erotic pilgrimage to the heart of her deepest desires.

Flight 69

Kelly Conway has never met a man like you read about in the story books. That all changes when she meets the handsome oil man James Swanson on the night flight to Houston and discovers they do things differently in business class.

The Secret Life of Girls

After the gardener spanks her bottom and a nun at her elite finishing school seduces her in the catacombs, Bella realises that sex was what she was born for. She adores wearing a dildo and deflowering virgins just as much as she adores indulging the roguish Christian Thomas with his addiction to fruit salads and bondage. Then Bella's world comes tumbling down. She learns that her beloved Ickham Manor doesn't belong to her, it belongs to her wicked stepfather. Sex has been fun. Now it is the weapon she uses to put her world back together again. Bella entraps her stepfather in a lewd act on video. She stars in a porn flick and, as her song on the soundtrack makes her a tabloid celebrity, Bella is at the beginning of an erotic ride into the showbiz world of pain and perversion, of domination and glorious submission.

Girl Trade

Emily feels wicked, liberated, daring. And bored. But her adventure begins on holiday in La Gomera, when a rugged beachcomber removes the leather thong from his neck and binds her hands behind her. Crossing oceans and continents in a nether world of smugglers, arms dealers, and pirates, she becomes the adored but captive jewel of the tough inflexible men who make a living in inhospitable landscapes. On hot afternoons on long days without number, she dedicates herself to the pleasures of sex in all its shapes and forms. She learns subservience. She becomes the perfect concubine. The perfect lover. She becomes Chengi - Girl.

Buy copies from Amazon or at my site chloethurlow.com